"Kristan Dooley invites us to journey into the unexpected. This invitation is the story of Kristan's life, learning to slow and turn left to follow Jesus off the beaten path and into the unknown. Here she opens the way to discipleship, challenging and encouraging us to grow and heal as we learn to trust the goodness of God wherever you are on the road of life, you'll find help here to travel to a new place with Jesus."

—Susan Carson,
Director, Roots&Branches Network,
Author of *Rooted (IN): Thriving in Connection with God,*
Yourself, and Others

"*Left Turns: Following Jesus off the Beaten Path* by Kristan Dooley is a compelling read for anyone looking to discover Christian discipleship as a grace-filled delight over against discipleship as a gruesome duty. Through the metaphor of left turns and uphill climbs, the author highlights the importance of allowing counterintuitive interruptions to become life-changing opportunities for spiritual growth. Insightful biblical exposition, personal illustration, and real-life application move discipleship from theory to practice. The author boldly invites readers to move off the easy road of discipleship to the costly but rewarding path of Holy Spirit obedience. I recommend, *Left Turns* for individuals and groups desiring to better embrace the call of the great commission to make disciples."

—David Sebastian,
Dean Emeritus, Minister at Large, Anderson University,
Anderson, Indiana

D1301903

"*Left Turns* gets me all excited for the opportunities Jesus has in store for all of us, if only we're willing to turn off the beaten path. Weaving her own story of turning left down a road only Jesus could see with examples from Scripture of how frequently God calls His people into the unknown so He can do His best work, Dooley provides a framework for all of us to listen harder, trust deeper, and move forward (or sideways) when God says it's time to turn."

—Laura L. Smith,
Christian Author, Blogger, and Speaker

"Kristan has mined the Scriptures for biblical truth that transforms our relationships. I am grateful she has combined her storytelling style with biblical scholarship to simplify complex thinking into manageable lessons. I welcome the invitation off the beaten path."

—Beth Guckenberger,
Author and Speaker, Founder/Director,
Back2Back Ministries

"Kristan Dooley is one of the most dynamic preachers and gifted authors I know. Both her speaking and writing come from a thriving relationship with Jesus with real-life stories woven throughout. I highly recommend *Left Turns* for every follower of Jesus. Truth is, if you have not experienced a left turn, you eventually will. If you are in the middle of a left turn, you need a lifeline. This book is that lifeline. It is insightful, engaging, and full of practical spiritual insights to help you navigate the turbulent waters of any left turn. Keep turning the pages. You will not regret you did."

—Tom Planck,
Chief Catalyst, Healthy Growing Churches

"If you have ever wondered what it would be like to live life off the beaten path, called to follow Jesus into the unknown, this book is for you. Kristan holds life with an open hand and in doing so, she has a freedom to work with the Spirit like few have ever experienced. Her journey is inspiring and not for the faint of heart. This is not a passive read. This is a change-your-life, put-on-your-hiking-boots, pack-your-backpack, step-off-the-pavement kind of book. God has a plan, and beauty can be found if you're willing to take a left turn!"

—**Crystal Colp,**
Pastor, Adult Discipleship, First Church, St. Joseph, Michigan

"These days, our lives are one left turn after another—left turns that have left us fearful and paralyzed. God has brought us a word of encouragement through Kristan Dooley. Kristan walks us through her left turns, turns directed by obedience to God and turns that come naturally with life. She helps us remember that God is there to walk with us. I was reminded that nothing I do or give makes God love me more. He just loves me no matter what turn life takes."

—**Shari Miller,**
Co-founder and Vice President, Made to Love

"We have all spent our share of time making our own path and what we thought was being alone as we did it. Kristan helps all of us understand that we are never alone, and even in those moments when we felt we had missed a turn, God was always there. Left turns remind us that there are powerful lessons in our time off the beaten path. Kristan helps all of us find lessons we might have missed in our journey as she encourages us with hers."

—**David Colp,**
Lead Pastor, First Church, St. Joseph, Michigan

"Kristan is a dynamic writer who has an incredible gift for putting language to the seasons of life that are difficult to find words for. The vulnerability expressed on the pages of *Left Turns* helps you see yourself in the story and calls you to the courageous path of following God even when life doesn't make sense."

—Sarah Davis,
Pastor, The Fringe Church

"It's impossible to know what to expect when you decide to follow Jesus. Some call it reckless faith; some describe it as a wild or dangerous adventure. What Kristan offers in *Left Turns* is a real-life account of obedience in the face of the unexpected awakening to God's grand invitation and the development of a disciple-making heart. I had a front row seat for the journey Jesus laid out for Kristan and her family: What seemed unguided in the process revealed itself to be masterfully architected in the end. In *Left Turns*, Kristan does what she does best: distills monumental learnings about the heart of the Father and the invitation for his children down to practical wisdom for those who are hungry and thirsty for more of God. This is a book for people who want to say yes to a flourishing life and who understand that the path may take some unexpected turns along the way."

—Luke Dooley,
President, OCEAN Programs

"Kristan has been working with us at Gravity Leadership for a few years now, and I can say definitively that she lives what she preaches in this book! Every lesson has been hard-won in the rough-and-tumble, messy practicalities of trusting God to guide and provide as we choose to follow Jesus in faith. Kristan's life is an icon of Jesus's teaching that the way up is down, less is more, and that turning 'left' is 'right.'"

—Ben Sternke,
Co-founder, Gravity Leadership

Left Turns

Following Jesus off the Beaten Path

Kristan Dooley

LUCIDBOOKS

Left Turns
Following Jesus off the Beaten Path

Copyright © 2020 by Kristan Dooley

Published by Lucid Books in Houston, TX
www.LucidBooksPublishing.com

ISBN: 978-1-63296-404-5
eISBN: 978-1-63296-415-1

Special Sales: Most Lucid Books titles are available in special quantity discounts. Custom imprinting or excerpting can also be done to fit special needs. Contact Lucid Books at Info@LucidBooksPublishing.com.

For my family

*Dave, Ella, and Addilyn, you have embraced so well this
hard and holy life of connection, intimacy, and ministry.
May our journey only grow deeper, stronger,
and richer as we press forward together.*

Table of Contents

Foreword

I am incredibly honored to write the foreword to this book. Kristan Dooley is a great friend and ministry partner. I have had the honor of leading with her all over the country through our partnership with Gravity Leadership. There are certain people who simply have the gift of communication. Take that and add her ability to change the atmosphere of the rooms she enters with the Spirit working, and exciting things always seem to follow. Kristan does this uniquely. I have learned countless lessons about who God is and who he is calling me to be from her, and I believe her to be one of the best communicators in our country. She has the ability to raise my faith a little every time I'm with her as she discerns God's presence. She is a disciple-maker who lives what she teaches. She knows God, walks with him, hears from him, and has the amazing ability to partner with him as he draws others into his goals and purposes.

I heard a teacher once say that "the fundamental principle of leadership is disruption," that the way we grow is simply by disrupting our normal patterns and rhythms and stepping off the path into something new. As I write this, I am drinking a Coke Zero. This will make Kristan laugh because she knows I have an on-again-off-again relationship with soda.

In fact, as I get older, I find that I need to disrupt so many of the patterns I love (cough cough, soda drinking.) These patterns were not a problem for me in my younger days, but now, if I don't disrupt them, they disrupt me.

It's a weird thing. For many years, I played basketball three nights a week, and I could eat all I wanted. I would stay fit and never gain weight. Then I turned 40, and things started to change. This year I turned 45, and someone from my church graciously told me I was now closer to 60 than I was to 30. The above-mentioned person has now been removed from all church invitations.

Not really, but when I turned 40, I broke my ankle for the fifth time, which forced me to retire from playing basketball. The truth is, my knees hurt terribly most days, and my gut grows each time I eat ice cream or a slice of pizza. I now gain weight simply by thinking about queso and chips. Suddenly, nose and ear hairs have appeared on the scene as if they had been hiding all of my life and just decided they want to see the world. I am sprinting toward gray hair, and though my wife tells me she loves the salt-and-pepper look, I wonder what she will think when it's all salt and no pepper.

I say all of this to illustrate what my body is teaching me. It's time to turn left, to step off the path I so easily traveled when I was younger. My future health and maturity depend on my present turn.

If we pay attention, our souls will also lead us forward in this lesson. Your left turn is important. You can't stay where you are and become the person you were created to be. What the world longs for at its deepest state are people who are fully alive. Yet often what it finds are people fast asleep at the wheel, doing what they've always done and merely believing what they've always believed. We are moving quickly and going nowhere new in our faith, experience, love, and understanding. Our lives may be lived in the fast lane, and though we are keeping up with the majority, we don't really know where we're headed.

Ephesians 5:14 says, "Wake up, sleeper, rise from the dead, and Christ will shine on you."

The invitation to turn left is an invitation to wake up and recognize that God is at work and there is more to this world than clocking in and clocking out each day. We're to wake up and realize every moment is ripe with the fruit of the Kingdom—to wake up and see the Lord is alive and he invites us to new life in him. To turn left is to taste and see that the Lord is good, and sometimes the tension disruption allows us to know exactly what will, in turn, help us grow.

My wife and I were invited by some friends to go on a marriage retreat a few years back. These invitations come often for pastors, sometimes making it easy to simply say no for fear of redundancy. The friends inviting us were wise enough to use the two code words that would get any pastor's attention—*free* and *beach*. Once we realized we received one free week on the beach, we easily agreed. It was winter, and we were living in Ohio at the time, which means it was cold and nasty. A free vacation and a chance to be together and connect seemed like a welcomed getaway.

We arrived, met some friends, prayed, relaxed, and listened to wise counsel for a few days. At the end of the retreat during a moment of ministry time, a man came to pray for us. He gave us a beautiful and terrifying prophetic word. "I see the two of you in a car driving into the ocean. The waves are beginning to pour over the car as you drive, but you keep your foot on the gas pedal and continue driving. Water begins to make its way into your car; it's knee-high, then it's at your waist and then your shoulders, and you begin to panic. You start banging on the windows trying to get out."

At this point, you can guess what I'm thinking—what kind of marriage retreat is this? He then looked us right in the eyes and said something that I will never forget. He said, "What you think is going to kill you is really going to give you life."

To be really honest, we were at the end of ourselves. When it came to ministry, it felt more like a death march than abundant life. We were exhausted, we weren't seeing the fruit we wanted, and truthfully, we weren't enjoying it much anymore. We were just going through the motions over and over again.

The word of the Lord got our attention. It broke something in us, leaving us both on our knees. We heard his word, but we still needed to walk in his word. Far too often we hear the word of God without ever learning how to walk in the word of the Lord. Returning home, we recognized that walking this out meant getting off the path, turning left, and following Jesus.

We had to *rise* up to meet him and awake from our place of sleeping. As we changed our perspective, our patterns, and our life rhythms, something remarkable started to happen. I could feel Jesus again. The Holy Spirit of God met us in a unique way that felt like both a disruptive tension and a healing presence.

My prayer as you read this book full of wisdom and challenge is that anything dead in you begins to move, pulling you toward new life. My prayer is for you to find the courage to step off the beaten path and into the arms of a loving God. My prayer is that you will recognize that God's calling is both better than you imagined and harder than you wished. It's both stretching and healing.

Wholeness is found on the other side of awakenings. Our mind gets awakened to the reality of God first, and then our body follows. The patterns we used to walk in seem insufficient, and what used to give us life seems lacking. It's in this space that God in his infinite mercy and love calls us to turn. He invites us to what's next. He calls us to dream again, and in the middle of all of it, he gives us our hearts back.

I don't know you, but I know this—you were created for more than the life you are living now. For every one of us, for the rest of our lives, there is an invitation to leave the path we have been walking and experience newness and nearness with the Father. Newness only comes on the other side of obedience, and resurrection comes only on the other side of death. This book is filled with encouragement, wisdom, and direction, which I pray will have you running toward your left turn.

I pray you find a new path, and I pray you find a new word. I pray the dead comes to life, hope is restored, and faith is strengthened. I pray that what you read in these pages awakens you to new life in Christ.

—Ben Hardman,
Pastor, Grace Marietta Church – www.gracechurchmarietta.com
Co-founder, Gravity Leadership – www.gravityleadership.com

Introduction

I was 18 the first time I stepped off the beaten path and turned left. During spring break of my senior year, I handed my beat-up life over to Jesus, wondering if he really could make something of my mess. I didn't know anything about real faith, but I knew it had to be better than this place where I found myself.

Weeks after I made this abrupt directional change, I sat at my kitchen table, surrounded by college applications, wondering how my new relationship fit into my future. My dream was to play college soccer, and I was well on my way. With offers from a few schools, it wasn't really a question of *if* I would play college soccer as much as *where* I would play it.

Shortly after narrowing down my options, my family and I made the six-hour drive to Murray State College to solidify my decision. That weekend I met the soccer coach and the team, toured the school, and did all but sign the papers of intent. It looked as though Murray State would be the place I would call home for the next few years.

I still remember the tension of the ride back home. My heart, which had faithfully loved soccer for as long as I could remember, seemed to have something new unfolding inside. My dreams led me to Murray State, but this new hope in my heart seemed to be pulling me somewhere new.

What should have been an easy decision suddenly felt complicated. I was very new at following Jesus, new enough to not even recognize his invitation to turn left. At this point, I didn't know that following him fully would come to mean a lifetime of stepping off the beaten path to embrace the unknown and unexpected.

He is so faithful to guide our path when we aren't mature enough to recognize we are following. I was days away from having to make a final decision when my friend and mentor, the one who led me to Christ just a few months prior, handed me a card. The message was simple and exactly what I needed to hear.

"When at a crossroads, always head for the cross."

This new love developing in my heart was pulling me in a new direction. I turned left and headed down a path I never intended. Instead of putting all my energy and time into playing college soccer, I redirected them in the way of discipleship. Instead of going six hours away for college, I opted for the familiar 40-minute drive to Miami University, Ohio and an opportunity to serve in my local church.

It took just a few hours on my new college campus to realize that I didn't know the least bit about following Jesus. But Jesus is an expert at teaching people to follow. He provided every step of the way. I was clumsy and new at this, and I got a lot of things wrong, but God was faithful to stay near, and at some point I seemed to find my footing.

Looking back at those four years and all the events that happened, I clearly see how they shaped who I am. They were pivotal in my formation and foundational in my faith. Would Jesus have shaped me while playing college soccer at Murray State? Yes, but he would have competed with my heart, my time, and my attention much more. Off the beaten path, he had full access to me, and by all accounts, he made the most of every second.

Since then, my life has been a series of left turns, each one with its own complications and celebrations. Sometimes, I've ignored God's invitation to turn in hopes I could keep traveling my current direction, and other times, I've turned with enthusiasm, knowing that where he led had to be better than my current place of residency.

Regardless of where my turns have taken me, one thing is sure—he's been the consistent piece in all this story, over and over again faithfully showing himself to be the best leader, the kindest guide, and the wisest mentor. It's become a story of friendship. The more I follow, the more I want to follow. I've yet to turn and wished I hadn't. Sometimes, it takes a minute, but all the time, it is good.

God is always there. Right turn, left turn, no turn at all, he won't leave. He can't. It would go against who he is. He is committed to you, faithful to keep inviting, faithful to keep pursuing, and faithful to keep loving.

You might know that. Maybe you've turned left a time or two and found him faithful. Maybe your turns, like mine, have formed and shaped you into the person you are today. If that is you, then I hope you know that there is still more ahead. And I hope your belief keeps you in a place of expectancy. The best relationships are those in which we never stop learning, never stop growing, and never stop knowing. It only gets better with time.

If you've turned left before and followed him off the beaten path, you will relate to my findings throughout this book. Maybe you've learned some of the very same lessons as you've turned. Maybe you have some to add. Either way, my prayer for you is that you get right in and open your heart to the prospect of a new invitation.

If you're new to this whole thing or struggling to turn for whatever reason, then you're in the right place. I completely relate to the tension his invitation may bring to your life. I also know the promises ahead should you choose to follow to this new place. My hope is that you find strength and encouragement as I let you in on one of my hardest but richest turns yet. I am not different from you. I've been scared, intimidated, anxious, excited, hurt, confused, shocked, bitter, and broken, but most importantly, I've been renewed. Whatever you are feeling, you are in good company.

Jesus doesn't travel like everyone else. His journey to save the world looked nothing like anyone would have expected. The disciples were constantly left with arms crossed and jaws dropped when Jesus, in step with his Father, suddenly changed directions. Still time and time again, they embraced what they couldn't see because of who they were coming to know, and it changed their lives.

At the end of the day, we find ourselves at another crossroads. Both roads cost you something. To keep moving forward at full speed has a price. To slow down and turn left also has a price. Will you open your heart and your life to what he has in store? Will you follow even when it's not what you expected? Will you go where you didn't ask to go and do what you haven't thought about doing? Will you turn, trusting that you won't get to the end of this journey and wish you hadn't come? I can't wait for you to turn left and follow him off the beaten path.

Part One

THE INVITATION TO TURN

CHAPTER ONE

Unexpected Invitations

Christlikeness is your eventual destination,
but your journey will last a lifetime.
—Rick Warren

It was early and freezing for a spring morning, cold enough to see your breath. I closed the front door behind me, hit play on my playlist, and set out for my regular run. I love to run; it's my escape, the place I go to get away. Weaving in and out of the running paths, I do my best thinking, my best planning, and my best praying. This is the place God has some of my best attention.

Nothing fights for God's space as I weave my way up and down the paths of our neighborhood. He has full access. To love running, you must focus on something other than the running itself. Counting the number of times your foot hits the pavement and comes back up again makes for a treacherous experience.

Rounding the corner, headed into mile four, I glanced at my watch to check my time—right on target and feeling good. As I approached my next turn, something began to stir on the inside. Pushing my way up the final hill, I felt the Father nudging me to turn left. It wasn't an audible voice. He didn't come through my earbuds or a bright split in the sky. I simply felt a quiet invitation deep inside whispering *turn left*. The more I pressed in, the more the words seemed to echo in my heart. *Turn left?*

I pushed back because I was confused. *Lord, are you asking me to turn?* It seemed out of sorts. Turning left wasn't really an option. I ran these trails every day, and I never turned left at this particular place. The path didn't go left. My five miles didn't need me to go left. I was right on pace to finish a little ahead of schedule. To my left were rows of new houses being built. It was a construction zone with hidden debris littering the freshly poured sidewalks. It wasn't a place to run, and worse yet, it was uphill.

When God invites us to turn, it is rarely about the circumstances around us and almost always about the connection within us. We tend to imagine following Jesus as an outside job when he clearly spends most of his ministry pulling us inside. Paul's prayer for the church of Ephesus has much to say about the inner work of the Father.

> *I pray that out of his glorious riches he may strengthen you with power through his Spirit in your inner being, so that Christ may dwell in your hearts through faith. And I pray that you, being rooted and established in love, may have power, together with all the Lord's holy people, to grasp how wide and long and high and deep is the love of Christ, and to know this love that surpasses knowledge—that you may be filled to the measure of all the fullness of God.*
> —Eph. 3:16–19

Internal Invitations

Turning left wasn't my issue; it was my invitation. The question in front of me that morning was simple: how was I going to respond. Would I let go of my plans and expectations and embrace the unplanned and expected?

As I contemplated God's appeal to turn, I realized I was already facing a different direction and headed up the hill. Something about being almost 40 frees you of the need to blaze your own trail. Throughout this journey, I've continually struggled letting go of my plans and surrendering to God's, but I wasn't put off by my dependency anymore. I've learned over time that only good things come when I follow Jesus.

Let's not mistake good things with easy things. Those are two very different ball games right there. Sometimes, God uses the physical to lead, guide, and direct the spiritual. What was happening physically as I began to follow this prompting off the beaten path would soon be presented spiritually in my life. At this given moment, though, I had no idea I would one day cling to this experience in hopes that God really would prove faithful in the midst of a left turn and a hard, uphill climb. God always gives us what we need to keep going, even if we don't know we need it yet.

The Trial of Trail-Running

When you run off the path and onto a trail, you are invited to embrace the moment. Your eyes need to be directly on the ground in front of you so you don't get tripped up. In this place, looking too far ahead becomes a dangerous way to run.

This was me turning left that morning. Eyes down to the ground, I stopped focusing so much on my future and focused on where my feet were hitting the present pavement. I've heard it said somewhere that the first half of your faith is learning to trust God with your past, while the second half looks more like trusting him with your future, and that seemed appropriate. To follow him into an unknown space would mean letting go of my current known space.

It wasn't hard to trust him with my past. For me, that was a given. I messed it up royally. If he thought he could fix it, then he was welcome to it because I knew there was nothing I could do.

My future, however, was something I held tightly. I had dreams, ambitions, gifts, and talents, and I wanted to use all of them to bring God's Kingdom more fully to the world around me. I had a family and responsibility. I had worked hard to follow God thus far, and I felt responsible for continuing forward successfully.

Making my way to the top of the hill that morning, I dodged debris, construction tools, and the mud puddles from the previous night's rain. I circled the cul-de-sac and carefully picked up speed, letting my legs carry me back down the hill. On the way down, I was able to catch my breath until I arrived back where I started, turning left once again and reconnecting with the familiar path to head home.

In the end, turning left cost me seven minutes. I reached my final destination and clocked more than the day's intended miles. The following afternoon, reflecting on my encounter with the Father, I asked for an explanation. What were his intentions? Was he trying to teach me something? Was there a deeper meaning? I know by now that his invitations don't usually come empty-handed. Revelation and understanding tend to follow surrender and obedience.

Here's an excerpt from my journal shortly after this encounter.

I'm going to ask you to step off the path. It's an unexpected turn in a direction that might not make sense. Your new road will be an uphill climb, littered with obstacles and potential dangers. Slow down, and watch your step. When you make it to the top, use the downhill stretch to catch your breath. With the wind behind you, your legs won't even notice the work as your body tries to keep up with the momentum gained. Then, just like that, you will be back at your path. In the beginning, it might feel like a lot, but by the end, you won't even remember being out of breath. And when you get to where we're going, you'll be farther than you intended to go.

Inevitably, if I had heard him correctly, a left turn was coming—and not just any turn. It was an uphill detour consisting of construction site debris, unpaved sidewalks, and uncomfortable breathing. He was about to invite me to turn and was gracious enough to tell me ahead of time so I could prepare my heart and adjust my posture.

Real-Life Road Decisions

Jump ahead with me about a year and a half later. It was mid-December, and I had just resigned from my job as one of the high school pastors at a large church in Cincinnati, Ohio, called Cincinnati Vineyard. After 10 months of preparation, I took the step and turned left.

Standing at the bottom of this seemingly impossible hill, I wondered what God was going to do now. Twelve years earlier, he called me into ministry, and I never looked back. I gave up my life as I knew it to follow him, only to wind up here, off the beaten path, in an intimidating and unknown alley.

Turning took me away. I was now walking (not running at all) in a perpendicular direction to what used to be my life. I turned, and everything else seemed to keep moving in the same direction. I struggled to make sense of how this fit into God's plan. How was taking me away profitable to the Kingdom? To my family? To me?

Transition is hard. To leave a place, even if you are headed toward another, is rough. Endings aren't always easy, and if we are honest with one another, rather than turn left, some of us resolve to make the most of where we are and who we are with. Even if it's hard, it's known, and there's something about the known that keeps us feeling safe and secure.

Throwing Things Off

Jesus came to give us life to the full, and yet many of us settle for half-empty at best. It does us no good to know him if we aren't going to follow him. I would even venture to say that if we aren't following him, it's because we don't really know him. His promises for us are perfect. His gifts are always good. We can trust when he leads. He leads as an invitation and not just because of an issue.

Sticking with the idea of running, I have a favorite pair of running shoes. Or maybe I should say I *had* a favorite pair of running shoes. Eventually, they stopped working for me, and instead of helping, they were hurting. They were my favorite because of the hours I spent in them. By month five or six, they were practically molded to my feet. They only became a hindrance when the soles became so worn that I could almost see through them.

At that place of security, I had a choice to make. Hang onto something that once fit perfectly or let go and move my feet into a nice (but not quite so comfortable) new pair of gel runners.

The Practice of Perseverance

In Hebrews, Paul says this:

> *Therefore, since we are surrounded by such a great cloud of witnesses, let us throw off everything that hinders and the sin that so easily entangles. And let us run with perseverance the race marked out for us.*
>
> —Heb. 12:1

This passage makes perfect sense when it comes to the second part of Paul's first sentence—"the sin that so easily entangles." Obviously, we need to throw off sin so we can run the race God has prepared for us. Where we get hung up is when the good things that used to be weightless and helpful are now feeling heavy and hurtful. Running up this unexpected hill with the Father would mean I didn't run it with my friends, with my job, or even with the dreams I had clung to most of my life.

Some of God's greatest gifts are unexpected. They are the ones we didn't see coming and the ones we hesitate to accept. They veer us away from the comfort of the old ways and into the unknown of the new.

The only way to accept these invitations is completely. We cannot partially follow Jesus to new places while wrestling to keep one foot in the old spaces. We have to surrender, throwing off anything and everything (good or bad) that is hindering us from the path God has for us.

I would be lying to you if I didn't confess that the tension of the turn caused some struggle. The unloading of resources and relationships in order to go in a new, unexpected direction brought a little bit of pain. The circumstances surrounding the turn unleashed some mild confusion, but the invitation pulled me forward. He never forces you to turn left; he only invites. Recognizing that he was reaching for me, I allowed God's Word to push my chair away from my desk as I surrendered my position, my security, and my dream to turn left and follow him forward.

Faith and Finish Lines

You don't get to the finish line of something you never start. Jesus's ministry had a start. There was an invitation, and then there was a turn, and just like that, he began walking a side street toward his future. It wasn't always easy. Read through the Gospels just once, and you'll see the persecution, hatred, lies, and misconceptions. But I believe that with just one glance at the disciples and their rabbi, you will find joy, connection, love, commitment, freedom, and security. They were faithfully united in their time together, and the depth of their friendship would forever impact their future.

Like it or not, the best relationships are forged on the hills of life. As we climb and battle and press forward, sometimes struggling to breathe, something deep inside of us changes, connecting us to the ones we journey with. The same is true in terms of your relationship with the Father. If we never struggle, then how will we find him faithful in the midst of hard things? If we never let go, how will we realize that he always holds on? If we never turn left, how we will learn to follow when we don't know the way forward?

The good news of the gospel is that we have the best guide. He is always present and always working, and he always has our best interests in mind. The journey off the beaten path is about learning to trust his leadership. It's about recognizing that he sees things from a different perspective. He has insight and wisdom that we don't. We don't understand his ways all the time.

Back Roads and Breakthroughs

For the disciples, the back roads Jesus took them on would build deep covenant relationships among them and their Savior. It's where they would discover a relationship so strong that not even death could separate it. Their connection would go on to impact generations of believers everywhere. In fact, their left turn is why we are here today.

If you've picked up this book, you are probably resonating with the idea of being invited somewhere. Maybe your invitation was unexpected, or maybe you've just been avoiding sending back your RSVP because you don't know your answer. Whatever the reason, you have a Father in heaven waiting to lead you off the beaten path and into new territory. There is a way to more than you've ever asked or imagined that only he knows.

The unknown is scary, but your hesitation is over because we can do this together. There is strength in numbers. Whether you are voluntarily stepping off the path or whether the road you've been traveling has been temporarily closed and staying on it is nearly impossible, it doesn't matter.

Don't let the enemy keep you idle when the Father has prepared your feet for walking. The people around you might not understand the turn ahead of you, but I get it. I've been there. I've stepped away. I've moved to the side and from that place I learned so much. I would love nothing more than for you to take my hand and let me help you turn, because, just like he had more for me, he also has more for you.

This is the journey of discipleship, the dive to a deep relationship and friendship. The disciples became disciples as they followed their rabbi.

Dallas Willard said, "Discipleship is spending time with Jesus to learn from Jesus how to be like Jesus."[1] The chapters to follow are what helped me as I journeyed to a new place. I wasn't taught how to walk through transition with a step-by-step manual. I don't think it's that simple. I learned as I walked, and so will you. You figure it out as you go with God, which means you will not find in these pages the exact picture of what will happen as you journey. But my prayer is that you will find encouragement in your turn. You are not alone. This is your journey to identity, freedom, and fulfillment. As the disciples followed Jesus, they learned, and they grew, and they became. And so will you. I promise. Let's find that story and turn to it together.

CHAPTER TWO

Side Streets and Back Alleys

If I want His promises, I have to trust His process.

—Lysa TerKeurst

It only takes one reading of the Gospels to realize that there is more at play than meets the eye. Right off the bat, readers and listeners are drawn to the hustle and bustle of the dynamic ministry being released through Jesus and his disciples. The towns are all abuzz, and the government is up in arms about the mesmerizing proclamations and life-transforming demonstrations taking place. Jesus appears to be rising in popularity with all the townspeople while equally becoming a threat to all the leaders.

Just before Jesus launched into full-time ministry, he was baptized in the Jordan River. Not even moments out of the water, he abruptly turned left and headed into what is often referred to as the wilderness. In the desert for 40 days of prayer and fasting, Jesus deeply centered himself in the love of his Father. His centering was extremely important because from this place of relationship, he would walk forward with his responsibility.

Jesus was fully human, and he would soon face and feel the fullness of his humanity. What he had stewarded in private, he would now walk in public. He would stand and overcome against all odds, but not in the way of the world. He would do it in the way of the cross. He would live a life of surrender and obedience, all in an effort to pave the way back home for us. Not for one second would he do this on his own. The responsibility before him was a by-product of the relationship planted within him.

It's the same invitation you and I have before us. Will we choose the road less traveled and walk the unpaved path? Can we go where others don't so we can embrace the fullness of the relationship into which we've been invited?

The Start of Something Real

Jesus called Simon and his brother Andrew to join him on his journey. Next were James, son of Zebedee, and his brother John. The men traveled to Capernaum where Jesus began teaching. His listeners were amazed at the words because he spoke as one who had authority and power. Jesus didn't teach them with fancy sayings and slogans. He followed his proclamations with powerful demonstrations, proving something greater was at hand. News began to spread quickly about this man from Nazareth, and everywhere he went, crowds gathered.

One of those first evenings, after ministry time, Jesus and his disciples left the synagogue and headed back to the home of Andrew and Simon. Upon arriving, they found the two disciples' mother in bed, sick with a fever. The Bible says that Jesus healed her, and immediately she got up and started cooking for them.

Side note: If I am sick or have been sick, it is to be clearly understood that we will be ordering take-out, quite possibly the entire week. Not so for Simon and Andrew's mom, though; Jesus touched her, and she went right back to cooking. Throughout the evening, people brought their sick and demon-possessed friends to Jesus, and Jesus healed them.

Praises and Popularity

Very early in the morning, while it was still dark, Jesus got up, left the house and went off to a solitary place, where he prayed. Simon and his companions went to look for him, and when they found him, they exclaimed: "Everyone is looking for you!"

—Mark 1:35–37

After a very successful day of ministry, Jesus got up early and snuck away to be with his Father. By the time the disciples found him, everyone in town was asking for his whereabouts. They wanted to taste his powerful words and experience his life-changing healing. It was working. The gospel was spreading. Jesus was growing in popularity. At this rate, he would win over the hearts of the people in no time.

There is a big difference between being chosen by God and being popular with people. Popularity was actually the farthest thing from God's plan. Sometimes, presence and popularity hang out in the same room, but often they are two very distinctive things. It took 30 years of my life to learn that being wanted and accepted by people paled compared to being favored and befriended by God.

Jesus walked so confident of this. He seemed free from the circumstances around him. Popularity was not on his mind. The messages he preached weren't meant to attract a comfortable crowd. He didn't mind a few squirming followers. In fact, he knew that discomfort is often what leads to the deconstruction of wrong beliefs.

Each time we come to know Jesus in a new way, we are faced with an invitation to live from a new understanding. How does our new knowledge impact our old heart? How does it change the way we see and ultimately become?

Jesus was there to raise the current level of awareness, to open blind eyes, to jump-start dead hearts, and to help the world see what it hadn't seen before. What he was sent to do would ruffle a few feathers. Dead people rising was bound to get a little uncomfortable. Jesus's identity, his confidence, and his calling weren't contingent on the applause and praises of his followers. If popularity were his end goal, his message would have never withstood all that lay ahead.

The way of Jesus is the way of the cross, and the path there is full of bumps and bruises. At times it feels isolated, somewhat intimidating, and littered with unknown shadows. But at the same time, it overflows with joy and peace, grace and truth, confidence and security. It is the way to life and life to the fullest. It is the only way we find him, and he is what we've been looking for all along. Alicia Britt Chole, author of *Anonymous: Jesus' Hidden Years . . . and Yours*, put it this way:

> Over the long, uncelebrated years while Jesus stewarded God-size dreams in anonymity, Father God had become his soul's true point of reference. That compass would serve him well as he walked into dry, troubled times.[1]

Early Morning Coffee

Look in the Bible with me at Mark, Chapter 1. After a long night of ministry, Jesus snuck away early in the morning to connect with his Father. I think it was because he wanted to but also because he knew he needed to. The townspeople wanted more, and while Jesus was with the Father, Jesus's disciples came to find him. Naturally, they wanted to answer the demands of the crowd. They were anticipating the quick growth of this new movement.

But listen to Jesus's response when Simon finally finds him, intending to bring him back to satisfy the crowd. "Let us go somewhere else—to the nearby villages—so I can preach there also. That is why I have come" (Mark 1:38).

Jesus turned left. The crowd was demanding his presence, and yet Jesus grabbed his friends, dipped down a side street, slipped out the back door, and moved on to the next place of ministry. He didn't stay on the rapidly forming highway; he didn't allow it to control his actions or dictate his response. He stepped off, almost as quickly as he had stepped on.

We would be smart to pay careful attention to the motive behind the move. Jesus, fully tuned in to the heart of his Father, did the opposite of what the majority of us would do as he picked his path. He didn't choose the way of crowd. He chose the way of relationship. He followed the invitation of the Father and faithfully stayed connected, even though it might lead to a bad critique from some confused townspeople. Jesus never reacted to the circumstances around him because he responded from the relationship before him. Staying connected to the Father was the most important thing.

I've changed my morning routine as my girls have gotten older. Ella wakes up at a quarter till six and takes about 30 minutes before she comes downstairs to leave for school. My alarm goes off at six. I get up, start the coffee, make sure the lunches packed the night before don't need anything added from the fridge, which allows just enough time for the coffee to brew. Then I grab a cup of coffee and take a seat in my spot on the couch. When Ella comes down, I'm all in for helping her get out the door. Usually, this involves heating up a cup of milk for some hot chocolate, going through the list of what she has after school, and checking off all the essentials she needs to leave the house with.

Ella leaves, and I then have 30 minutes before it's time to wake up Addy and do it all over again. And guess what I do next. Nothing. I do nothing. I sit down with my coffee, and I might read my Bible, go through a study, finish up the chapter of whatever book I am reading, or just sit there. But I breathe, and I linger. I check in with God and with myself. And it really does change my entire day. Rushing through my morning throws things off-center for me.

The Real Thing

Why would Jesus follow the Father off the beaten path? What empowered him to go against the grain? How could he just drop the needs and wants of all those people back in town? These questions have to get our attention. There was something there, off to the side in the alley that was more important than the wants of those people—something significant.

What Jesus found was the most important thing. It's the thing for which we were created. He found relationship—the real thing. It's not the impressive, quick version but the deep-rooted, lasting kind. Relationship is the reason God calls to you and invites you off the beaten path. It's why he pulls you away from the crowd and why finding the courage to turn left is one of the most rewarding things you will ever do.

Jesus didn't travel the highway. It wasn't about all he would get done (although he would accomplish a lot) as much as it was about who he would come to know. Jesus came for the people. He came for you and for me and for the person sitting next to you on the bus or walking through the grocery store wearing headphones. He's real and really personal. He's big and yet so small, both at the same time. So because he's after relationships with real individual people, our journeys won't all look the same. What he has for me is not the same as what he has for you, and where he leads you, he won't lead me. There are some turns we might take together and others that we will not.

Regardless, this is the story of the gospel, the truth of Jesus making his way into a town, offering everything, and yet at the same time holding onto nothing. It's the good news for each of us. It is our invitation to rescue and redemption, our promise of freedom.

Jesus invites you into a storyline that will forever change your life. The only catch is that it takes your entire life. Will you follow when he turns, even when it doesn't make sense, even when you have to set down whatever is in your hands? Can you walk away from the crowd and lay down your need to belong, your desire to fit in, or your fear of being unknown? Can you put relationship before responsibility?

I think you can, and I also believe you want to. You know deep down that relationship is calling. You might have been meaning to answer for years, but stepping off the path into the unknown is intimidating. Follow Jesus long enough, and he will tell you to turn left because he wants to know you more. He has something to show you in those back alleys, something to tell you on those side streets. There's more to him than meets the eye and more for you than you ever imagined.

It Will Twist, and It Will Turn

Jesus's life with the disciples proved to be one of unexpected twists and turns all the way to the very end. Had the disciples only gone where they were comfortable, they would have missed the best of what Jesus had to offer. Instead, they mustered up the courage to turn left, step away from life as they knew it, and embrace the unknown with Jesus.

Off the beaten path, they found the life they never knew they needed and yet always longed to have. Off the beaten path, they became learners listening to the words of their faithful rabbi, teachers mimicking the works of their leader, and world changers compelled not by the culture around them but by the commitment within them.

If we got the chance to ask the disciples, Jesus's closest friends, what their favorite memories were during their season of ministry with him, they would tell us things that we've not read about in the Gospels. Sure, they might mention the feeding of the 5,000 or the time Peter walked on water. They might talk about the events they later shared on stages or around dinner tables year after year, but mostly, I think they would laugh at their inside jokes and give each other a hard time over conversations we've never even heard about.

I think they would make eye contact with one another in agreement and that we wouldn't even begin to understand all they experienced. And they would encourage us to turn left and find out ourselves. Depth happens on side streets. God isn't pulling you away from the world as much as he is pulling you into his presence. I believe we were created to turn effortlessly, that our spiritual maturity can be measured in the amount of time it takes us to turn and follow Jesus in a new direction. The side streets and back alleys are where relationship is forged, and my prayer is for your participation. I pray you realize you've been promised goodness and that he who promised it is faithful.

CHAPTER THREE

Firehouses, Prostitutes, and Drug Addicts

His glory is good gifts that often look small and messy and a head-scratcher economy where we lack nothing as long as we surrender everything.

—Shannan Martin

I realize that these three topics—firehouses, prostitutes, and drug addicts—came out of nowhere. But as random as they are, they were exactly what I encountered as I started my uphill climb. Since I had just turned left and resigned from my job, I wondered what this side street would look like for me. Where were we going? What was God doing? Were we going to be okay?

Jesus is a fan of spaces and places. If he is leading you somewhere, it's because he has something to give you. He could have given the disciples the keys to the kingdom and their inheritance from heaven those first few minutes of their invitation, but he didn't—not because he didn't know how they were going to grow. He knew Saul would eventually become Paul and that Judas was never going to make it to the end. He knew enough to not need the journey, but the journey wasn't about him; it was about them. These everyday, ordinary men needed time and trials and testing to forge a friendship that would withstand the winds of the world. The relationship was dependent on the journey.

I met Daniella at a Panera restaurant after a social media conversation brought us together for an unknown reason. This is a normal practice of mine now, meeting up with people I feel drawn to but don't know why. But back then, it was something new. We exchanged stories, shared what God was doing in our lives, where we were, and how we were struggling to figure out his plan.

At some point, something I said sparked a connection inside of Daniella, and she proceeded to tell me about an old, abandoned firehouse and her call to prayer and worship. Through a series of events, the Father had given Daniella an incredible vision. It was of Hose House #4 on East Avenue in Hamilton, Ohio. This old, beaten-up, broken-down firehouse sat next to a homeless shelter, a halfway house, and a brothel. It was smack dab in the middle of the red light district on one of the worst streets in the city, and yet in her spirit, Daniella felt an invitation to transform it into a house of prayer and worship.

All of this was just a dream until she "accidently" met the guy who owned that old firehouse. The man had big plans for his fire station, but not for the next five years. In five years, he would retire and begin to rehab Hose House #4 into a beautiful space, but for now he was happy to hand over the keys and allow Daniella to make good use of the place.

I had to make sure I hadn't missed something important. It seemed too easy. I said to her, "Wait! God gave you this dream, you somehow met the guy who appeared to hold the keys, and he just handed them over to you, free of charge, for the next five years?"

"Yeah," Daniella confided in me. "That's basically where I am right now, trying to figure out what it means to take the keys and build this ministry." We continued to talk about what her next steps might be until it was time for me to leave.

I didn't make it far, two miles down the road at best, when I picked up my phone and called my new friend. "I'm in!" I shouted. "If you want to do this, I will help you. I don't really know what street ministry looks like, but I'm willing to figure it out as we go." If quitting my job was my left turn, Hose House #4 felt like it might be my hill. Little did I know this would become the place God gifted me in order to receive more of him than I knew possible. Here I would unload my baggage, find my healing, and deeply connect in friendship with my Father.

Here We Go

Three months later, on Easter weekend, Daniella and I opened the garage door to Hose House #4 for our first worship experience. It was a long, crazy road from there with stories we could never fully retell. We had no way of communicating with our neighbors. We couldn't send out a church-wide email to the homeless or those living without electricity. What worked for ministry at the mega church would not work here. The bells and whistles would actually drive people away. Hose House #4 was unfinished and broken down in every aspect, and learning to embrace the reality of the broken actually seemed to be our invitation.

This side street would set me up to build a relationship of trust with the Father in a way I never knew possible. In that old, broken-down firehouse, I found my footing in the most unexpected way. I realized that I am able to walk anywhere as long as Jesus is my guide. The best things I bring to the roads I travel will never be the position I play, the performance I make, or a sermon I deliver. The best thing I can do for the world around me is to learn to carry well the presence of Jesus within me.

Home is a state of being and not a place of arrival. It had to be or I wouldn't have felt more at home in that old, beaten-up place than anywhere else in the world. There I found healing and wholeness, faith and freedom. I learned to trust and love and let go of what I could not control. Hose House #4 was a place of renewal and transformation for my weary heart.

Life in Rhythm

We launched into Hose House #4 knowing we had to create a rhythm of being together for worship, prayer, and community. The only way to teach our neighbors that we would be there was to actually be there. So on Wednesdays, Fridays, and Sundays, we threw open the heavy garage door, pulled out some old donated patio furniture, and worshipped. Sometimes, we had friends available to lead us, and sometimes we didn't. It never made a difference. It wasn't really about how we worshipped; it was simply about worship.

Friday nights, we had a sound system and an open invitation from the brothel next door to plug into their electricity. I'm not kidding. Our next door neighbors ran a brothel, and we borrowed their electricity and worshipped our King.

I will never forget the night a man came out of the brothel trying to talk on the phone. Worship was loud, and I thought he was surely coming to ask us to turn it down. He looked at me, smiled, and then made his way to the street corner where he could hear more clearly. The people next door never once asked us to turn it down—not once.

Hose House #4 was busy and loud—loud worship, lots of praying, people and addicts walking the streets, police sirens, passing trains. You name it, if it was noisy, it was probably happening while those doors were open. Sunday nights were for prayer. We kept the garage door shut and invited people into a much needed quiet space. Sometimes our neighbors showed up, and sometimes they didn't. Either way, we prayed.

My favorite person at Hose House #4 was Richard, who lived next door at the halfway house. He was an old war vet, and he loved to tell stories. The first day I met him, I heard every detail about his leg injury. Richard was almost always outside when we pulled up. In the past, pulling up to a building where I would soon hold a service of any type would make me think of all we needed to finish before we were ready. But it wasn't like that here. There were no programs or projects, just people.

The uphill climb of my left turn was teaching me that it wasn't my job to fix every person I encountered. I was not the sum of what I had to offer. My job was to be present. I think Jesus would have listened to Richard. He would have leaned in closely and paid attention to the details of his Vietnam days. He wouldn't have been thinking of what to say to get him saved and waiting for Richard to finish so he could get a word in about what was most important. He simply would have been available.

Richard made it clear to me from the very beginning that he wasn't coming to our "church." Church wasn't for him. Still, he was always outside waiting for me before we arrived, and he always let me pray for him before we left. One evening while we were gathering, I was in the back praying with someone when out of the corner of my eye I saw Richard walking in front of the Hose House. He appeared to be pacing back and forth, coming closer and closer with each stride.

By the time I said amen and looked up, Richard was standing next to me, inside our church, as he always called it.

"I think I need you to pray with me," he said.

"Okay, Richard. What about?" I asked.

"I just think I need to be closer to God," he said as he shuffled his feet, keeping his eyes on the ground below us.

"You know what, Richard? I think God wants to be closer to you, and I think He's simply waiting to be invited. I have an idea. Why don't you pray, and I will stand here and help you if you need it."

Richard took his beaten-up war hat off, bowed his head, and began to pray the most humbling, soft, broken prayer I've ever heard. It was golden. We hadn't offered Richard anything but Jesus, and in the midst of that, Richard found everything.

For the first time in my life I wasn't trying to fix the person in front of me. I was surrendered to just being present. I didn't pastor him or guide him or try to get him to be any different. I simply met him there in his unbelieving reality and let it be okay. And look at what happened. He came forward, looking for Jesus.

When Proximity Is Your Offering

Here's a truth we have to understand. As sons and daughters of a really good Father, life isn't about what we bring to the table. It's not about how good we are, how hard we work, or how much we have or don't have. It isn't about where we fail or where we need to work harder. My goodness does not lead to God's kindness. His kindness actually leads to my goodness. Our offering is in showing up just as we are and partaking in his goodness.

In the beginning, it was hard to be available two to three times a week for the Hose House and to give up every Friday night. But very quickly it just became what we did, and doing it brought us so much life. We gathered together at the Hose House again and again until the Lord brought me back to my old path of church leadership and led my husband, Dave, and me to plant Anthem House Church with our long-term ministry friends from early on.

At first, I had no idea why I was where I was. Why the turn? What was God doing? Where were we going? I kept insisting I had something to offer. I kept trying to do what I had always done. I started the ministry at the Hose House thinking we would change the community, only to realize that the community would change me.

God's love bid me to come and receive, to open my hands and walk in his grace. He taught me to be a child, completely dependent on the provision and power of her Father. He taught me that I could ask for things because I wanted them and not only because he needed me to have them. He sat down at the table with me and showered me with his kindness, and I did nothing but soak it in. He taught me that a life well lived is not about performance or perfection; it's simply about presence and participation. He taught me to breathe, to rest, and to slow down and release the pressure to do more, be better, work harder, and go farther.

And he wants to show you that, too. It's why you've felt prompted to turn left time and again. What he has for you is too important for him to give it to you in a drive-by. He values it too deeply. If you step off, He will step in, and what unfolds might change you forever.

CHAPTER FOUR

Twists, Turns, and Transitions

The desert is not intended to be their final destination but rather a necessary middle space where they will be formed as a people and established in their connection to God.

—Jeff Manion

It's the story woven throughout the Bible—God inviting his people to turn left and follow him into new territory. Even Jesus wasn't exempt from a left turn. After his baptism, prior to launching his earthly ministry, Jesus turned left and headed into the desert. He battled uphill as he fasted for 40 days and nights, depending on his Father to be his food.

He hadn't eaten for more than a month when Satan first approached him and said, "If you are the Son of God, tell this stone to become bread" (Luke 4:3). In the Greek texts, "if you are the Son of God" can also be translated "since you are the Son of God." Satan wasn't tempting Jesus to show him what God might do; he was tempting Jesus to show him what God would do. They both knew God was able.

First, Satan offered Jesus bread to quiet his appetite. The temptation was to reduce what Jesus needed to mere physical substance and thus satisfy his hunger. Had Jesus turned the stone to bread, it would have been a fear-driven reaction to not having enough rather than the faith-driven response we see as he trusted God to be enough. Living meant so much more than food, clothing, and shelter. Sure, he needed these things, but there was something more that he needed. Jesus knew living wasn't just about having.

The desire to have enough isn't wrong in and of itself. It simply becomes an idol when you step out from under the umbrella of the Father's provision and seek to secure life yourself. I don't know what security looks like to you. I tend to find security in the people around me. Do I have everyone I need? Do those people (the ones I need) have everything they need?

I definitely battled this on my uphill climb. Shortly after I resigned from my job at our Cincinnati church, my husband, who was also employed there, was let go. We saw the writing on the wall long before it happened. God was doing a new thing in our hearts, and as a family, it was important for us to travel this road together. But things got real when Dave lost his job and was promptly turned left. He was without work, I was without work, our family was without health insurance, and we didn't know what the future would look like. The pavement under our feet ceased to exist.

The temptation on the last day at our church would have been to have a plan in place of what "next" looked like. It would have been to take control, to make something happen with or without God's involvement, to shore up the ground upon which we walked. Instead, we walked out of the building, shook off the dust, piled into the truck, and headed for a week at the lake. This new season was not one we would figure out; it was one God would usher in.

The Pull of Security

In the beginning of our time at Hose House #4, people came asking for things. They needed food, money, and clothing, and their needs were legitimate. It opened my eyes to how we as a church have created a system to meet physical needs instead of mend spiritual hearts. At this point, Daniella, Dave, and I had all left our jobs, and we honestly didn't have much more to offer. The neighbors didn't know how to take it when we didn't hand them something but instead invited them somewhere. I can offer you nothing but myself and my time. Would you come?

It took time for them to trust that our invitation was genuine. The longer we consistently opened the garage door, the more they lingered. When Jesus was in the desert that day, he had food to eat that the enemy didn't know about, and in that old, dilapidated building, we might have just found that same food.

Living with an unhealthy need to have enough leaves you missing the opportunity to rest in his enough, and thus you are robbed of the peace promised for your journey. Suddenly, you work and live to experience security rather than work and live from God's security. Your decisions are based on making sure your needs are met instead of what God will do to provide for your needs.

Jesus silenced the devil this way: "It is written: 'Man shall not live on bread alone'" (Luke 4:4).

The Power of Significance

Next, Satan hit Jesus with an opportunity for quick approval. He said the worship of all Jerusalem would catapult Jesus and his mission on earth, quickly bypassing the need for any road development and landing him straight on a six-lane freeway. This was Jesus's spiritual home, the focal point of his faith. People were looking for someone to lead them away from the oppression of the Roman government. No doubt Jesus would use their instant approval for good.

The enemy has a strange way of disguising God with good. The message Jesus carried was meant to gain traction with people through real relationships and the spreading of grace and truth, but here, the enemy offered it to him instantly and painlessly, served up on a silver platter. All Jesus had to do was hand off his affection for the Father, and people everywhere would be talking about him, following him, and worshipping him.

> *The devil led him up to a high place and showed him in an instant all the kingdoms of the world. And he said to him, "I will give you all their authority and splendor; it has been given to me, and I can give it to anyone I want to. If you worship me, it will all be yours."*
>
> —Luke 4:5–7

Sometimes, we overlook Satan's craftiness. The lies of the enemy aren't overt and obvious. They come as twisted versions of truth, subtle ideas tainting your motives and distancing you from the heart desire of the Father. Satan wasn't offering Jesus something he wouldn't have. One day, every knee will bow and every tongue will praise Jesus in heaven and on earth. It's going to happen. Jesus is going to be all everyone will talk about. The enemy's offer was just a manipulation of the way it would happen and the road they would travel to get there.

The enemy wasn't trying to get Jesus away from his calling. He was simply trying to persuade him to walk it out in a way that wasn't defined by freedom. This is the disguised power of captivity, and it is often why Jesus invites us to step off the path and spend time in the alleys, deep-diving into a relationship with him.

Again, Jesus stood strong in his place of identity. "It is written: 'Worship the Lord your God and serve him only'"(Luke 4:8).

I totally relate here. I had years in ministry, teaching on a stage, using my gift to bring people closer to Jesus—all the while allowing it to stabilize me in a place of significance. If I had something to offer, it would secure my seat at the table. If they approved, maybe God would approve.

Jesus knew that Kingdom significance isn't about what he had to offer. It is about what the Father has given. What Jesus did didn't make him who he was. He was not just as good as the sum of their applause. So again, he refused the enemy and stood his ground, trusting God to move him forward in due time.

The Need of Belonging

Last but not least, Satan takes Jesus to the highest point in all of Jerusalem and tells him to throw himself off the cliff so all of God's angels can rescue him. From this place, everyone in town would see that Jesus was part of something much bigger. He would instantly have thousands upon thousands of followers. No one would doubt the power and authority he carried, and everyone would want to be part of his team.

Over time, the world would witness God's power displayed through the resurrection of his only Son. Satan was just fast-tracking Jesus to the end game. "Here," Satan might have said, "do it on the highway in front of all the people—quicker, easier, cleaner." The enemy was offering Jesus a way in. Perform for the people, and they will choose you. Show them who you are as a way to earn their favor. Use your pull to gain their presence.

Jesus answered Satan, "It is said: 'Do not put the Lord your God to the test'" (Luke 4:12). And with those final words, the enemy walked away defeated. Jesus stood strong in the face of insecurity, insignificance, and a lack of belonging. He didn't give in to the enemy's offer.

The same enemy who sought to lure Jesus onto the highway of identity works in our lives through the same subtle lies. He's asking you to win the approval of others through your strengths. He's threatening you that if you don't work all hours of the day, you will lose your place in line. He's taunting you that if you don't give your kids the latest and the greatest, they will fall behind. You are not meant to be driven by his idle threats and temptations and thus see yourself as less than you are.

Your effectiveness comes from your connectedness. You know your identity because you know your Father. It was Jesus's secret. He didn't need what the enemy offered because he already possessed it. The devil does not have the authority to take away who you are. He only has the ability to skew the way you see yourself and the inheritance that comes with your identity.

Satan lives in pursuit of keeping you on the highways and byways because the trials and tests that form you unfold on side streets and in back alleys. He throws significance, security, and belonging around like confetti, pulling you to stay comfortable where you are rather than risk following Jesus as he leads you off the beaten path and into a new identity and freedom.

The Friction of Freedom

Adam and Eve weren't placed in the Garden of Eden with demands and restrictions. They were placed there with purpose and power. God welcomed his beloved creations to their new home and told them to be fruitful, to rule over all the fish of the sea and animals on the land. He put them in charge and gave them authority and a place to be creative. The garden was not a place of imprisonment but of freedom.

Isn't it funny that the enemy made the garden appear restricted? With just a subtle shift of words and a few quirky remarks, Satan took what was so good and made it appear so bad. He took what should have felt limitless and made it seem limited. Adam and Eve were not being controlled or constrained through the one thing God asked them not to do. They were being protected. They were given a choice. Would they choose to live in the freedom gifted to them, or would they focus on the friction of the one thing not included?

What you face becomes what you embrace. Adam and Eve faced the bad news, the one thing with the power to separate them from their Father and enslave them to the world. When we know whose we are, we can't be convinced of who we aren't. Adam and Eve had everything, yet they lacked self-awareness. They were sons and daughters of God with full access. They were not limited until they bought the lie that something in this world had more to offer than the Father of this world, and with one bite, everything changed.

It was the same for the Hebrews as they tried to escape their slavery in Egypt. God heard their cries and sent Moses to their rescue. Through many miracles and devastating plagues, the Egyptian leaders fully experienced the power of God. The straw that broke the camel's back was when the angel of death swept through Egypt, killing the firstborn of every family that had not covered their door with the blood of an innocent lamb.

Pharaoh's firstborn son was dead, and in Pharaoh's grief, he quickly sent the Hebrew people on their way. God's people were well on their way to freedom when they heard the sound of pounding hooves behind them. Pharaoh had changed his mind. Egypt was nothing without its slaves. The Hebrews stood with their backs to the Red Sea and their fronts to a failed future.

As they stood before the oncoming army of Pharaoh, they quivered in their sandals and quickly forgot whose they were. The same God who rescued them from Egypt was still in their presence and able to do it again. Had they just turned around and looked at the waters of the sea as their invitation instead of their issue, they might not have crumbled.

But just like Adam and Eve saw what they didn't have, the Israelites immediately jumped to the worst-case scenario. The people cried that Moses had brought them out into the desert to die. They said they were better off as slaves and should just go back.

Still, even in the midst of their panic, God was faithful. He rescued them in their unbelief. He parted the waters, led them through the Red Sea on dry land, and crushed Pharaoh's army underneath the waves. Then he turned them left once again and led them on a journey called freedom.

God will lead us left as many times as necessary. It's what He did for the Hebrews, literally. He walked them in circles over and over again in pursuit of a real relationship. He loves us too much to let us go forward without it. Your left turn, your alley, your desert (however you want to refer to it) is not your issue. It is your invitation.

Responsibility and Relationship

In the Gospel of John, Jesus tells his disciples, "I no longer call you servants, because a servant does not know his master's business. Instead, I have called you friends, for everything that I learned from my Father I have made known to you" (John 15:15). At this point, Jesus and the disciples had taken many turns together. In fact, they were in the midst of the biggest, most unexpected turn yet. Jesus was headed toward the Garden of Gethsemane where He would be arrested and eventually crucified. It was more important than ever that his disciples know that this was a relationship because religion would never lead them in the direction they were meant to go.

Our responsibility is birthed from our relationships and not the other way around. We aren't slaves working for our freedom. We are children living in freedom. But so often we fail to see the inheritance we've been given. You can't live in the freedom and abundance of your Father and at the same time live in slavery to the world around you.

"No one can serve two masters. Either you will hate the one and love the other, or you will be devoted to the one and despise the other" (Matt. 6:24). We serve what we believe. That day in the Garden of Eden, with freedom all around them, Adam and Eve decided to believe the lies of imprisonment. They entertained the lie that a simple piece of fruit would bring them more of something they actually already had, and they took a bite. From their choice, chaos and confusion crashed onto the scene, and the struggle has been real ever since.

Our core beliefs dictate our conscious response. Either we will slave away working tirelessly to gain something already written into our inheritance or we will rest confidently as sons and daughters working freely from the gift we've already been given.

God plans for you involve walking in victory, but the road there isn't a smooth highway. He never wanted slaves; he wanted sons and daughters. And since that day in the garden, he has been in pursuit of reestablishing what was taken away.

After the waters of the Red Sea had calmed and any signs of the drowning Egyptians were long gone, God turned his people left to begin their journey home. It was meant to be a much shorter trip to the Promised Land than you might have guessed. What took the Hebrews 40 years should have only taken them about 11 days. God never meant for them to spend that long on their side street. What he had done for them physically he wanted to do for them spiritually, but it was their choice to participate or not.

There is an invitation we must accept should we desire to live as sons and daughters. We must choose to believe our Father and build our relationship. To really believe something is to set our hearts to it, and not just our minds. Learning to embrace something in our hearts takes turning left. We must travel off the beaten path with the Father in order to know we can trust him with what we don't know. Depth like that cannot be learned; it has to be experienced.

My Left Turn

My left turn was about joining Jesus. It was our time together, stepping into something that would change us forever. It was about freedom, a reclaiming of the land, a renewing of the mind. As I walked away from all I had become, I was given the chance to embrace the empty space of who I really was. In this new space, I was not only the sum of what I had to offer, I was the daughter of all he had to give.

Serving is funny like that. We were created to serve. In fact, we are called to it all throughout scripture, but the place from which we serve is of utter importance. We must serve from a place of identity and not for a place of identity. We already have all we need, so we can give to others freely.

What I do, where I serve, and how I live cannot confirm who I am. When it does, it leaves me continually doing, serving, and living from a place of unrest and need. In this place, I live with a constant search for security, significance, and belonging. From this place, I survive, controlled by the outer circumstances of life instead of thriving from my inner securities.

This was my story, and I didn't even know it. In the same way, some of the Hebrews didn't understand the full extent of their bondage. And just as Adam and Eve forgot about all the other trees in the garden, I had missed the deception of the enemy. He slyly slid false motives and misrepresented intentions into my life that kept me working for meaning and performing for acceptance. I spent my time walking in circles, hoping to move myself into an inheritance my Father was trying to freely hand me all along.

My left turn was the exact in-between I needed. It took me away from the beaten path and onto a side street that would forever change the way I interacted with my Father.

In this place I learned that love was not greater when I did more, and it wasn't less when I didn't. In fact, it wasn't based on my performance at all. It was always there, always ready, and always waiting to be received. I learned that God works in my whole life and not just in the parts of my life I thought mattered to him. He's my dad, which means my entire life matters to him. He enjoys me, delights in me, and wants to spend time with me, even if I'm not proving my worth and value. I learned that the goal of our relationship was not to get things done but rather to be together. He didn't need me to work for him. He was actually capable of doing all things without my help. The invitation to join in was about keeping company.

Comings and Goings

Jesus left the desert the same way he entered, fully confident and secure in his identity. He was the Son of God, and from that place, he would move forward. It's the invitation you have before you, but you won't find it on the highway. The formation of friendship and identity happens off the beaten path—in the back alleys and on the side streets where you encounter his goodness in ways you haven't earned and in places you could never deserve.

Jesus's life with the disciples proved to be unexpected twists and turns all the way to the very end. Had they only gone where they were comfortable they would have missed the best of what he had to offer. Instead, they mustered up the courage to turn left, to step away from life as they knew it and embrace the unknown of Jesus.

Sometimes, God pulls you away from the world so he has space to pull you into him.

I believe we were created to turn left effortlessly, that our level of trust and connection leads us to freely follow. Your spiritual maturity can be measured by the amount of time it takes you to turn and follow Jesus in a new direction.

My prayer is for your participation—that you realize you've been promised goodness and that he who promised is faithful. The story of the Hebrew people is simply a sad story of a group who never really believed what they had been promised. Relationship is your invitation. The side streets and back alleys are his direction.

CHAPTER FIVE

The Shadows in Your Alleys

*The Lord is looking for those who are so in love with Him
that they will say yes when they are wooed and still say yes
when great sacrifice is required.*

—Heidi Baker

There was an alley at Hose House #4. My kids weren't allowed to walk through it by themselves. During the day the alley was open and felt secure, but in the evenings, it was full of shadows and darkness, making it a bit scary. Because there wasn't any running water in the Hose House, we had to put a port-a-potty out back behind the building. The only way to get there was through the alley. As if that wasn't intimidating enough, we had to wrap a chain around the port-a-potty and keep it locked when no one was using it because people would use it as a place to shoot up heroin whenever we weren't there.

You can't make this kind of stuff up. The alley was a place of transition. We used it to get from one place to another. We didn't linger there because the shadows of the unknown were intimidating, but we embraced it as part of the journey.

We all have alleys in our faith, and even though we would like to avoid them, they are necessary for our growth and development. If you have hopes of not always being where you currently are, then you need to find the courage to embrace the unknown journey through your alley. If we are going to follow Jesus off the beaten path, then we are going to have to come to terms with our alleys.

The disciples had to deal with their shadows—the lies they believed about themselves, their Father, and the world around them. They had to navigate their alleys long enough for Jesus to shine his light of truth into the darkness. Light has a way of revealing the broken truths under which we've placed ourselves. Part of knowing what we believe is also knowing what we don't believe. The alleys tell us the truth about our beliefs.

If Dave and I said we trusted God with our future but shook in fear at the loss of our jobs and walked forward in angst and anxiety, seeking to secure our lives the best we knew how, our alley would reveal our true belief—that we trusted in ourselves and our jobs for our security. Losing those meant that we had lost our grounding.

So with this new revelation, we have two choices. We can leave the alley, get back on the highway, find security in something, and move forward. Or we can stay put, linger in the alley, press through the uncomfortable feelings and the tension of surrender, and learn how to trust.

Stepping off the beaten path forces you to pay attention to your footing. The foundation upon which you stand is vitally important. The world is unpredictable. Circumstances change in an instant. The wind was so strong last night that I lay awake in bed for two hours listening to it whip and whistle. When I drove to the gym this morning, not a single trash can was still standing. Some were even in the middle of the road. Tree limbs and debris lay scattered in almost every yard. I even saw a few trampolines folded over because they could not withstand the storm.

Wind is unpredictable. It comes, and it goes. If you aren't in the middle of shifting circumstances, it's only a matter of time before the wind blows them your way. Jesus himself said that we cannot put our faith in the world. "In this world you will have trouble. But take heart! I have overcome the world" (John 16:33).

We have been gifted with the ability to navigate the storms of life. When our current path crumbles right before our eyes, there should be a solid foundation of truth and grace waiting there to keep us steady. Turning left is about testing this foundation. It's where you stop saying it and start being it.

How does God feel about you? What are his promises to you? How does he move? Where does he go? How do we follow? His presence is in every alley, so we don't have to fear. The light always overcomes the darkness. It's not a question of whether we will make it. You will get through the struggle of your alleys. He will not fail you.

Hiding in Shadows

You know what's crazy to me? When Adam and Eve misstepped and ate the apple, they immediately hid from God. They withdrew and went dark, or as my 15-year-old daughter would say, *they ghosted*. No one told them to do this. No one was before them demonstrating what to do when you mess up. To hide was simply their instinct.

The enemy is good at what he does. His lies will pull us into the darkness and separate us from God's goodness if we don't learn that part of overcoming the shadows is recognizing that a shadow is only a shadow because of the light. Think about it for a minute. If there were no light, there would be no shadow. Shadows exist because light exists. Essentially, every shadow will lead you back to the light if you wade through it long enough.

The problem is, shadows come in all shapes and sizes. Some of them are new, and others we've lived with our entire lives. They have been there so long that we wouldn't recognize our world without them. Shadows are lies we believe about the Father. They are the places we plant our feet. In basketball, as long as you keep one foot planted, you can move the rest of your body around as much as you like. It's called pivoting. When we plant our feet in the shadows, we pivot our lives from there.

What we do is affected by what we believe, and oftentimes, the speed of our lives does not allow us the option to slow down long enough to realize where we are pivoting from. More times than not, we say one belief with our mouths and pivot from another in our lives.

My Shadows

Here's what you have to know. There was a level of belief in my life. My family and I dedicated our lives to living our faith out loud. I trusted God. I believed in him. I worshiped him. I loved him. But there was still more. There was more to him than I knew.

Have you ever had a friend who was just a friend until one day they became so much more? Something happened, the fog cleared, and suddenly this person is more like you than you thought. You now see them in a different light. Your conversations are deeper, they are stronger, they are sharper. You confide in her and she in you. There's a connection that encourages you and moves you forward.

Relationships take time, and healthy relationships develop more as time goes on. It's natural to grow closer to the Father over time. There is more to him than you thought you knew. There will always be. He is infinite, and his goodness will never be completely understood this side of heaven. That being said, no matter where you are, there is more of him for you to know—more of him for you to trust, more of him for you to love.

When Worship Looks Like Wrestling

The shadows in your alley, those lies you don't want to deal with, can be seen as your issue or they can be seen as your invitation. There's a story in the Old Testament that I love. Jacob actually wrestles God for a blessing. Jacob was one of the sons of Isaac and Rebekah. Jacob has a messed up story. His older brother, Esau, was favored more by their father, while Jacob was favored more by their mother. When their father was near death, he asked Esau to hunt and kill some wild game for him to eat with the promise that when he returned, he would bless him.

The Old Testament blessings of a father included promising words of inheritance and prophesying the future. It was a coveted thing. While Esau was out hunting, Rebekah helped Jacob disguise himself and trick Isaac into giving him the blessing instead.

When Esau returned home and discovered that his little brother had weaseled his way into their father's blessing and his large inheritance, Esau set out to kill Jacob.

Jacob took all he had and ran away. He lived with Laban for 20 years before deciding to come home and seek to restore peace with his big brother. As Jacob returns home, he does so with as much respect as possible. He was seeking restoration, not war, with his brother. As an act of faith, Jacob sent his family and all his possessions home in front of him.

That night while Jacob was alone, scripture says he wrestled with God.

> *So Jacob was left alone, and a man wrestled with him till daybreak. When the man saw that he could not overpower him, he touched the socket of Jacob's hip so that his hip was wrenched as he wrestled with the man. Then the man said, "Let me go, for it is daybreak." But Jacob replied, "I will not let you go unless you bless me." The man asked him, "What is your name?" "Jacob," he answered. Then the man said,*

"Your name will no longer be Jacob, but Israel, because you have struggled with God and with humans and have overcome." Jacob said, "Please tell me your name." But he replied, "Why do you ask my name?" Then he blessed him there. So Jacob called the place Peniel, saying, "It is because I saw God face to face, and yet my life was spared." The sun rose above him as he passed Peniel, and he was limping because of his hip.

—Gen. 32:24–31

Three things stand out to me about this passage. First, even though Jacob had the blessing of his father, he was still searching for contentment. He longed for that which he actually already had because the way he went about getting it was force and manipulation. In the end, he got what he wanted, but it didn't get him where he wanted.

There was still something missing. He was still living in the shadows of his older brother. And he could stay in those shadows, pretending he had all he needed and go about his life as though this was as good as it gets. He could deny the ache in his heart for something more, or he could turn left, come home, and deal with his deceit.

The second thing that stands out to me is Jacob's persistence. Jacob wants to be blessed by God. He knows there is an inheritance for him as a son, and he is willing to fight for it. I remember a conversation with one of my mentors in the middle of my shadows. I was struggling to understand why God had me at Hose House #4. It just didn't seem to fit with the direction I thought I was headed.

I was okay with being there; I just didn't understand how to be there. Do I just let go of everything else and make this my new life? Do I stop writing and teaching and surrender to being a street missionary? Did I have it all wrong all this time, and were all of those pictures and promises in my mind for someone else?

I was definitely wrestling with God. In my wrestling, I was also hearing the voice of the enemy. Do you know how I know it was the voice of the enemy? Because it was condemnation and shame. *You shouldn't be struggling with this. You should just surrender and obey. Why are you spending so much time trying to work through this? Why can't you just submit and do what God has asked you to do?*

Over and over again, the record playing in my head cut me down—until my friend helped me see that the wrestling wasn't the issue. We can wrestle as we worship. I wasn't wrestling with God because I wanted to do something and he wanted me to do something else. I was wrestling with him because I wanted to do what he wanted me to do. I was wrestling as worship.

God isn't offended when we seek to understand. In fact, I think if he knows we will be able to understand, he will not withhold such insight. Scripture says, "No good thing does he withhold" (Ps. 84:11). If understanding is good for us, then understanding is what he will give. And if it's not, then in our wrestling, we might find that he is asking us to move forward, even though we don't understand.

Jacob was wrestling as worship. He wanted the promises of what God had for him, and he wanted them fully. He was going to press in no matter how long it took. In my search for understanding, I was never seeking to build a case for why I shouldn't turn left. I was seeking to understand what I needed to surrender so I could turn. Those are two very different ways of worshiping.

When you think about the invitation the Father has issued to you, are you wrestling in worship or wrestling in worry? Are you seeking to understand what needs to be released so you can move more freely through your shadows, or are you trying to keep hold of what you want so you can feel better in your shadows?

Finally, it would be good to know that Jacob was physically impacted by his wrestling. For the rest of his life he walked with a physical reminder of this spiritual battle. He was changed. Often when we wrestle with the Father, we too come out changed. God has a way of shining through on the other side of our wrestling. When his light overcomes our shadows, we are not the only ones who notice. Other people will benefit from the time we spent wrestling our shadows. Our families will feel the light, and they will notice the change. They will reap the blessings.

I will never forget the day my daughter Addilyn asked me to dance at the Hose House. It was only week two, and we were just getting started. I was still very uncomfortable with what the Father was doing in and through my family. We gathered in a circle with some of our new community and began to sing worship songs. Addilyn is not my dancer. She's a soccer player. She's rough and tough and tends to stay away from the things her sister loves, like dancing and cheerleading. So when she asked me to dance, I was caught off guard. But at the same time, it made the moment feel even more like Jesus.

"Mom, will you dance with me?" she asked in her sweetest seven-year-old voice possible. As she asked, she pointed to a few other people who were in the back of the room dancing to the worship music. I twirled her around a few times before I sent her over to my friend Diane. I knew Diane would dance with her. I knew she didn't care what other people thought. I knew she had a level of freedom I hadn't found yet. Addilyn and Diane spent the rest of worship dancing in the back together, and I spent the rest of my time pressing into the Father.

What was it in me that denied this invitation? Why did I feel like I had to say no? I spent much of my teenage and young adult years out of control. In fact, it had taken me so long and I had worked so hard to regain control that to simply throw it out the window for Jesus felt almost a little counterproductive. Part of growing up was learning to control myself, and yet part of growing down seemed to be learning to let go of this control.

In my wrestling to understand, I felt the Father speaking to me about letting go. He said something like this: "These battles you

I want this for my children

fight will bless your kids. They will stand on a different foundation because of the work you are doing. They won't have to unlearn wrong paradigms the same way you had to. They will simply know the truth, and the truth will set them free."

I felt so encouraged. I wasn't just wrestling for myself. I was wrestling for my family. The people around me were going to reap the benefits from the connection forming within me. Jacob had to have felt that as well. He wasn't just returning home for his own benefit. He had a family. The restoration of his relationship with his brother would not only benefit him, but it would benefit his entire family.

You will turn down streets and wrestle with shadows, and other people will benefit from your effort. That's the gift of the gospel. In fact, it's the gift I hope to give you in the rest of this book. The next seven chapters are shadows I've wrestled with in my alley and the truths I've discovered in the midst of my fight. My prayer is that you will benefit from my battles, that the work I've done will make your alley a little less intimidating. I know because that's my story. I only had the courage to turn left because I witnessed countless people in front of me following God into impossible places, and part of me longed to know him like they did.

There are people who will benefit from the time you spend wrestling, and that's a promise. So wrestle in worship, not worry.

Part Two

THE INVITATION TO TRUST

CHAPTER SIX

God Is Always Present and Always at Work

The Gospel is good news for eternity, but also for now.

—Bill Johnson

E lla's eyes darted up and down the rows of parents. From the stage, everyone was probably in the dark, and it was extremely difficult to tell one person from the next. Still, I knew who Ella was looking for. Finally her eyes met mine, and I knew she would stop searching and breathe. She danced for so many people that afternoon, but something about our connection and my presence in the audience enabled her to rest in the midst of her first performance. There is no better audience than an audience of love and acceptance. It's a stage from which you don't have to earn applause or approval because you know you already have it.

If you have kids, you know what I am talking about. "Mom, watch. Dad, look. Mom, Mom, Mom, did you see when I. . . ." Our children live to know we are present and tuned into their lives. They want our eyes, attention, assurance, and approval. Our applause has the power to silence a hundred critics.

Addy loves that I love watching her play soccer. After most soccer games, she gets in the car, excited to run down the list of things she did and didn't do during her game. "Did you see that cross, Mom? What about that shot?" Whether she played the game of her life or struggled to follow through isn't as important as my consistent presence.

My girls know I am cheering for them on their best days just as loudly as I am cheering for them on their worst days. My praise doesn't have anything to do with their performance. I love them no matter what they do or don't do. This love gives them the freedom to go for it without fear.

They are not a product of their performance; they are people of their relationships. And from the place of relationship, what they do has little hold on who they are.

From the Beginning

From the very beginning, the Father wanted relationship. Listen, he is not simply in this for what he can get out of it. He is not looking for a bunch of puppets who will do whatever he has commanded. He would give up the world to have a relationship with you. He already gave up his Son. He wants a real relationship, something that is just as real as the person sitting next to you.

God created us to be his children. The idea from the beginning, in the Garden of Eden, was to live in a perfect relationship with him. Before sin, we could coexist with God, walking with him and talking with him. From this place of connection, we are invited into freedom. There is nothing we need to do in order to solidify more who we already are.

Genesis says that Adam and God walked in the garden together. Sin interrupted that perfect union with our perfect God. When Adam and Eve made the choice to eat from the fruit of the forbidden tree, they opened themselves up to an entirely new audience. Instead of only hearing the applause of an adoring Father, they now heard the chatter of constant critics. This change dramatically affected them. But one thing remained the same: God never changed. He still longed to be with his people, and he stayed their number-one fan.

Later, in order to make himself more accessible to his people, God came to Moses and gave him the instructions to build a tabernacle—a tent of meeting. This was the place where the presence of God would live. It was the place God's people could be aware of his consistent presence in their lives.

It's quite possible that Moses and God reflected this relationship best. Moses knew God, and Moses loved God—and he loved being with God. The Bible says Moses would go into the tent, and the presence of the Lord would fill it. God would talk with Moses face to face, like we do with each other. Moses regularly experienced the fullness of God.

Then the cloud covered the tent of meeting, and the glory of the Lord filled the tabernacle. Moses could not enter the tent of meeting because the cloud had settled on it, and the glory of the Lord filled the tabernacle. In all the travels of the Israelites, whenever the cloud lifted from above the tabernacle, they would set out; but if the cloud did not lift, they did not set out—until the day it lifted. So the cloud of the Lord was over the tabernacle by day, and fire was in the cloud by night, in the sight of all the Israelites during their travels.

—Exod. 40:34–38

It's crazy to me that the Hebrews lived aware of the presence of God but chose to keep themselves distant from the presence of God.

They could see the tabernacle, they witnessed the cloud, and they even followed the cloud. But they never asked for the experience they watched Moses have. They settled for experiencing God through Moses.

This is exactly why it doesn't work for us to only know God through someone else. God's relationship with Moses wasn't enough to keep the Hebrew people on the straight and narrow, and it's not enough for us either. Over and over they struggled to follow and obey. God was leading them to a land of promise, a land of abundance, a place where all their needs would be met. They had witnessed the length to which God would go for them, but their struggle to know him and to trust him turned an 11-day trip into a 40-year journey.

When we settle for only ever knowing the God that lives through other people, we walk in circles, unable to ever truly know ourselves. If my girls never heard how much I loved them and never experienced my celebration of them as my daughters, they would stop listening to my voice in their lives and start living from the words of others.

God is our Father, our really good and really present Father. He cannot be compared to our earthly fathers. He is perfectly present and always working in our lives. We are always invited to recognize and respond to his work.

New Testament Tabernacle

God's promise didn't change because the Hebrews couldn't get out of identity crisis mode and trust him. Essentially, he is a father, and his heart is at home in relationship with his children. God's longing to be with us and our inability to simply receive his presence ultimately led him to the gift of his Son. Jesus became the physical tabernacle.

And the Word became flesh, and did tabernacle among us.
—John 1:14 YLT

Jesus became the physical tabernacle and dwelled among us. Jesus lived with God's people. He was the real, breathing representation of God—God in the flesh. He carried the full power and authority of the Kingdom of heaven on earth. Being in his presence was the same as being in the presence of God the Father.

Jesus was access to God without all the pretension and religion. No wonder crowds flocked to him. No wonder people laid down their lives to follow him. It's no doubt they clung to his every word. He was fully human and yet divine at the same time. God was in their midst. The one they were created to know was there and wanted to know them.

Everything changes when Jesus walks into the room. Imagine the way your response shifts when Jesus walks through the door by your side. Picture the way you interact with your friends—the things you say, the things you don't say. Think of the hope you bring to those struggling in hopelessness when Jesus sits down at the table with you. Suddenly, nothing is off limits; nothing feels impossible.

Jesus changed everything for the disciples. On their own, they were unschooled, ordinary men, but with Jesus, these 12 men changed the future of the church. The presence of Jesus affects everything it touches. To walk hand in hand with Jesus empowers us to walk differently. Just like Ella needed to know I was present at each of her performances so she could perform from a place of rest, we have to know the presence of God is available to us in our everyday, ordinary lives. It's not something we have to work for as much as it is something we get to live in.

Holy Spirit Presence

And here's the thing. Jesus walked around with people in the New Testament days, but walking around with them for the short time he was on earth was not enough. Jesus couldn't be everywhere with everyone, and he wouldn't stay forever. God intended to reach the ends of the earth, and to do that, another helper—Holy Spirit—was needed.

The Father sacrificed his Son so we could be with God always, not in a far-off, distant, rule-following religious way but in an up-close and personal-relationship way. Our identity doesn't have to be found outside in a tent or through someone else. It doesn't even have to be found in Bible study or at church. Our identity actually lives within us.

> *Don't you know that you yourselves are God's temple and that God's Spirit dwells in your midst?*
>
> —1 Cor. 3:16

The presence of the Father lives in you. He literally tabernacles inside of you. He has set up a tent in your soul and given you direct access to the only identity you will ever need. We are not wayward orphans walking about trying to find a home. We are beloved sons and daughters with the gift of home right in our very beings. Part of knowing who we really are starts with recognizing who God really is.

The Israelites experienced God in the tabernacle.
The disciples experienced Jesus as he tabernacled with them.
We experience the Spirit as he tabernacles inside of us.

Perhaps the greatest prayer we can pray is not the prayer for God to deliver us from the circumstances threatening to control our identities, but instead a prayer for God to deliver us into his presence, which promises to hold steady our identity in the midst of our circumstances.

> *But if Christ is in you, then even though your body is subject to death because of sin, the Spirit gives life because of righteousness. And if the Spirit of him who raised Jesus from the dead is living in you, he who raised Christ from the dead will also give life to your mortal bodies because of his Spirit who lives in you. . . . For those who are led by*

the Spirit of God are the children of God. The Spirit you received does not make you slaves, so that you live in fear again; rather, the Spirit you received brought about your adoption to sonship. And by him we cry, "Abba, Father." The Spirit himself testifies with our spirit that we are God's children. Now if we are children, then we are heirs—heirs of God and co-heirs with Christ.

—Rom. 8:10–11, 14–17

Whoa! That's good. Christ living in you changes everything. Your identity will never come from something you do or say. It comes only from who Jesus is and all he's already done. Learning to recognize his consistent and available presence in your life is the most important part of understanding who you are.

We recognize those we spend time with. The disciples knew Jesus because they spent large amounts of time with him. When everyone else was still busy trying to figure out who Jesus was, they were certain he was the Son of God.

I know the voices of my girls because I spend large amounts of time with them. I can pick their laughs out of almost any room. Likewise, I know when a cry for help is real and when it's a worked-up version of an overtired child. The ability to recognize them lives inside me.

The Power of the No-Bake Cookie

Dave's grandma made the best no-bake cookies. Mamaw Mary, as we called her, passed away years ago, and none of us have been able to duplicate the texture of her no-bake cookies. They were perfect in every way. I was the last one to realize their perfection. Believe it or not, I thought no-bake cookies were something I wasn't interested in. I mean, who eats a cookie you don't bake and, worse yet, one with chunks of oatmeal poking out all around it. Talk about looks being deceiving!

One year, standing in front of our Christmas dessert table, I reached back behind me and grabbed what I thought was a chocolate chip cookie. Without looking, I put it in my mouth. I was shocked to bite down and realize I had not grabbed a chocolate chip cookie. At that moment, the no-bake cookie became the best cookie to ever exist. It was just the right amount of rich mixed with this weird yet satisfying texture of oats, causing it to basically melt into my taste buds. From that moment on, the presence of no-bake cookies made a dramatic difference in my life.

If they were in my house, I struggled to not respond to them. I tried everything I could to put them out of my mind. At one point, I remember getting out of bed in the middle of the night, sneaking across the cold wood floor trying not to wake the rest of my family, and enjoying a no-bake midnight snack. And I thought about them in the basement when I was on the treadmill. Their presence would convince me that running one extra mile created the space for two extra cookies. I would hear them calling to me while I was upstairs just before the girls got home from school, knowing that if I ate them now, I wouldn't have to share them later. Their presence was everywhere, and it was all-consuming.

In fact, I loved those dang cookies so much that the following year, instead of one box at Christmastime, Dave's grandma gave us two. One for me (because, let's be real, they lasted me about three days) and one for Dave who has more control than I do and can savor those suckers for a month. I put my hand on Dave's box. "If you know what's best for you, you will hide that box somewhere that I would never look. Don't pull them out in front of me, and no matter what, don't show the kids. They will sell you out in a second."

The presence of those no-bake cookies changed everything in my house for those few weeks. And yet if I am honest, I have to admit that there have been weeks in my life that the consistent and constant presence of Jesus impacts me less. There have been moments when I have passed up the presence of Jesus to stay in bed. I've overlooked

sad but true

what Jesus was doing to finish what I had planned. And I've not stopped and submitted to his invitation because of the way it would impact my day or the day of those around me.

God is always present and always at work. As his child, I have a standing invitation. I don't have to scan the crowd to see if he is paying attention. I can be confident that he's there. I can be sure he sees me. I don't have to create a good play in the game so I can keep his attention. He wrote the playbook, and he has called me to run point. I don't have to beg him to come into the room. I simply get to wake up to the fact that he is already there.

> *Here I am! I stand at the door and knock. If anyone hears my voice and opens the door, I will come in and eat with that person, and they with me.*
>
> —Rev. 3:20

I turned left and encountered a shadow in my alley that told me that the more I accomplished for God, the more I would enjoy him. This shadow left me on a stage performing for his attention, scanning the audience for affection. What I did, I did in hopes he would notice, and I would know he noticed because he would do something significant in my life. I often begged him to show up, and when he did, I ran myself ragged hoping he would never leave. It was exhausting and never enough. *Not good at all*

All the while, he was standing at my door knocking. He was present the entire time, in every mundane moment. He was there when I woke my girls up in the morning, as we walked to school each day, and again when we said good night. He never left.

Broken Spaces and Beat-Up Ideologies

Remember that side street in the city of Hamilton where I found a little beat-up building without much to offer? Inside that space, I found the fullness of everything I needed. The Father was there, and it wasn't because of anything I had done. He was there, and I wasn't having a mountaintop experience. His presence was tangible, and yet I wasn't running around like crazy because of all the work I had to do. He was there, and I was doing nothing.

All this time, I thought it was what I did that got Jesus's attention and brought him near. I had to stop doing so I could start seeing. He is near because of who he is and not anything I do. His commitment to me isn't about me and my inadequacies or me and my need for perfection, or me and my struggle to connect, or me and my fears, doubts, or insecurities. His commitment is about him. He is committed because of who he is, not who I'm not.

Nothing I could do would change the reality of the Hose House #4 space. Sure, we raised money, washed windows, found furniture, and cleaned the place up. I think we had it looking pretty inviting for a run-down building with no electricity. But our efforts didn't make the Father more comfortable. He was right at home in the midst of what wasn't done. His presence isn't found in our work as much as it is in our rest. And sometimes, our left turn involves a slowing of pace, because to move forward into what we don't know, a stronger revelation of who he is, is necessary.

Worship Night Wanderings

I have a favorite night at the Hose House. It was a Friday, and a group of friends from another Hamilton church came to lead worship. The space was packed. Dozens of people crammed into that little building, singing and worshiping the Father in a powerful way. Our kids were running around, mosquito candles were burning, and behind the scenes, the sirens of the street were blaring.

I looked around and realized that on the highway of my life, I never would have put myself on this street with these people. This was not something I saw coming. I had little in common with others in that room, and yet at the same time, I never felt more connected in my entire life. The common denominator wasn't church, it wasn't worship, it wasn't prayer style, and it wasn't teaching ability or a Bible degree. It wasn't anything anyone brought to the table. The common denominator was Jesus. It was his presence. Connected to him, I felt connected to them.

His presence is the secret ingredient in all relationships. We know this, but in our actions, we are far from living it. We work hard to be in relationship with others, and we should; other people deserve our best. But what if Jesus is the thread holding all things together and our time is better spent being together with him? Maybe finding him in the room and figuring out what he is doing would transform our frustration into favor. If God is always present and always working and I am always invited, then it's not about me and the work I am doing. It's about my living a life that puts me in proximity to him and what he is doing. It's knowing and recognizing the presence of the Father and doing whatever it takes to lay down what's in my hands to link arms with him.

It's getting out of bed in the middle of the night, opening the door he stands knocking at, pulling out a chair, and listening to all he longs to tell me. God's presence never shifted when my workload changed. He was steady when my emotions were high. He was consistent when they dipped down low. He was always there. Whether I was working hard and producing well or struggling to face the very next day, he was there. In fact, during my season of struggle—that off-the-beaten-path journey away from my job and onto the side streets—his presence seemed all the more near.

The presence of the Father in your life is not based on what you do or don't do. It's based on who he is. He is steady for you. He is consistently consistent with you. He is there, right now, in your space. The question is, can you slow down long enough to notice him? Will you put yourself in places and spaces where you will recognize his invitation more fully? Are you willing to lay something down so you can pick him up? This journey isn't about asking him to show up. It's about learning how to wake up to an always-present, always-available Father.

CHAPTER SEVEN

God Actually Likes Me

*We cannot assume that He feels about us the way we feel
about ourselves—unless we love ourselves compassionately,
intensely, and freely.*

—Brennan Manning

Jesus was present for me in my nothingness. He was also there in my everything. It just took having nothing to see him as everything. You don't have to keep trying to obtain his presence. He is already closer to you than you think, and that simply never changes. God's design from the very beginning was to be with us. The Garden of Eden was about relationship and intimacy.

God doesn't "show up" because He's already present. Saying he "showed up" assumes he was not there and then he was.[1]
—Gravity Leadership

Sometimes when I am struggling, I hand my car keys over to my feelings. I will break this down a little more in another chapter, but for now, just know that when my feelings get behind the wheel of a car, they tend to drive me to Target. Maybe you've seen this Pinterest post: "One does not go to Target knowing what they want. One goes to Target to allow Target to tell them what they want." When I felt alone and couldn't stand the stillness of my house any longer, I often wandered the aisles at Target.

After my left turn, I stepped into an alley that left me alone a lot. Having worked at a church in full-time ministry almost since the day I handed my life over to Jesus, I wasn't used to being by myself. There had always been something to do, some event to plan or team to lead. In this cold alley, I was alone.

No one was cheering for me. No one was watching. There wasn't a crowd in sight. The noise of my life died down, and the stillness brought me to a new place. With all my time, Addilyn and I fixated ourselves on Joanna Gaines on the *Fixer Upper* TV show. Something about watching old things brought back to life gave me such hope. There were many nights we watched two or three episodes, sometimes ending with me in tears.

I was particularly drawn to the little wooden cutting boards Joanna placed in every finished kitchen. They always caught my eye, and I secretly wanted one. Never mind that I didn't really like to cook or that I already had a plastic cutting board. The idea of a nice, chunky, wooden cutting board sitting on my counter made me happy.

Sometimes, I would go to Target in search of a wooden cutting board. Maybe I found one, maybe I didn't, but either way, by the time I finished meandering through the aisles, I would convince myself that when you don't have a job and don't really like to cook, you don't buy unnecessary cutting boards. Then I would take the keys back from my feelings and drive myself home.

Trust was not easy to come by. I literally felt like I picked my foot up to walk, not knowing if the ground would be there when I put it back down. In my loneliness, I felt unknown and unseen. Knowing that God was working even when I wasn't was harder than I imagined.

You Can Worship while You Wander

On Friday nights, our family went to Hose House #4 for worship. This particular week, we were running late. By the time we got there, worship had already started. As we walked down the sidewalk, my new friend Ed came walking toward us.

He had a strange look on his face and something behind his back. The minute I was within reach, he started talking, "This might seem weird to you, but I am a woodworker, and sometimes when I am out in my shop working on things, I feel like God puts people on my mind. He doesn't do it all the time, but when he does, I always feel like I am supposed to give whatever I'm working on to the person he is bringing to mind. You might not want this at all but . . ." And before he went on, he pulled out the most beautiful wooden cutting board I have ever seen. It was thick and checkered with different stains of wood. And it was handmade by a friend I had met on this side street.

But most important, it was a gift from my Father who loves me and sees me and wanted to remind me that he is there, he's working, and he's got this. God was present even in my wanderings. He saw me at Target. He knew the emptiness in my heart. He felt the ache, and he made himself known to me. He filled the void just like he's always promised.

Tears streamed down my face. I know both Ed and my family thought I was crazy. I took the cutting board and told him exactly how much it meant that he brought this particular item to me. And in that moment, for the first time, my mundane exceeded my

71

mountaintop. It did. Right there on my side street, the place where I felt I had nothing to offer, I found that God still had everything to give. My always-present Father came near, and the experience surpassed every great accomplishment I'd had up to that point.

To say that God is always present and at work is only Good News if the God who is present and at work is good.[2]
—Ben Sternke, Gravity Leadership Academy

I was beginning to understand that God's countenance didn't change according to what I was or wasn't doing. He has an eternal smile on his face where I am concerned.

Missed Marks and Measurements

I wonder if the disciples ever worried about a disgruntled Jesus. Did they wonder if their struggles pushed him too far? Were they concerned that maybe their last slip-up might be the end of his patience? Did they try to make him happy by working to outdo one another in an effort to gain his affection?

We see a little bit of this when the mother of James and John asks Jesus to grant her one wish, that her sons would sit next to him in paradise. The desire to be near Jesus wasn't the issue. We all want to be next to him. We were created to be next to him. Even the disciples, who were walking with him, wanted to somehow be closer to him.

No one ever told me God smiles at the thought of me or how he delights in the very thought of me. I am seriously the apple of his eye, his little daughter whom he couldn't love more. I just didn't think he liked me. I don't know why I didn't think he liked me. No one told me that he didn't, but somewhere along the road, religion left me feeling like I didn't measure up. My lack of good works left me on the wrong side of a much needed relationship. I didn't know God's nearness was not dependent on my goodness.

I remember struggling as a new believer trying to put one foot in front of the other most days of my life. The more grace I needed, the less grace I embraced. I didn't know how to do this faith thing, let alone do it well. My failures left me with the picture of a far-off Father instead of a faithful friend.

Full of shame every time I failed, I gave God the space I thought He wanted. I sometimes went weeks without praying, not because I didn't want to but because I thought I didn't deserve to. It was punishment. If he would not punish me for my failures, then I would do it for him. Rather than humble myself and receive the love he offered, I prided myself and rejected the grace I needed. But in my back alley, I encountered a God who actually wanted me in the family, even on my bad days. A. W. Tozer said, "What comes into our minds when we think about God is the most important thing about us."[3]

I think Jesus really liked his disciples. I think they were friends and family. I think he thought about them as he went to the cross. This wasn't an arranged friendship; it was a chosen friendship. Jesus didn't do it because he had to. He did it because he wanted to.

"For the joy set before him, he endured the cross, scorning its shame, and sat down at the right hand of the throne of God" (Heb. 12:2). With joy He went to the cross because he knew what would happen on the other side. On the other side of this hard turn, the gift of right relationship would be readily available for everyone. No more gimmicks and rituals were necessary to come before the throne, just God the Father, Christ the Son, and Holy Spirit, fully ready and available for unrestricted relationship.

Slaves and Servants

I considered myself a slave for Christ. I would work for him and work hard, constantly coming back to him asking what I could do next. But slavery is not what he's invited me into. In fact, in John 15, Jesus looked at his disciples and said, "I no longer call you servants, because a servant does not know his master's business. Instead, I have called you friends, for everything that I learned from my Father I have made known to you" (John 15:15). Jesus knew what they didn't. They made far better friends than servants or slaves.

Slaves serve because they have to, while friends serve because they want to. The two are driven by entirely different motivators. That is why I love that Jesus gave Peter the keys to the Kingdom of heaven (his inheritance) right after what he would consider an epic fail. Simon Peter didn't have enough faith to stay on top of the water because his surroundings got the best of him, and he couldn't keep going. I can so relate to the disappointment he probably felt. But Jesus didn't even mention it when, in the very next chapter of the Bible, he changes his name to Peter and tells him he will be the rock upon which the church is built and hands him the keys to the Kingdom of heaven.

Does that sound like a disappointed dad to you? You don't give your house keys to someone you don't want in your house. Jesus didn't choose Peter because of his success rate. He chose Peter because of a depth of relationship. It wasn't that Peter successfully walked on water; it was that Peter willingly got out of the boat. Jesus wanted Peter in his house in the same way he wants you. You don't have to read far in the Gospels to be inspired by how Jesus meets people. His story is a story of love.

He drank water from the woman at the well and had lunch with Zacchaeus, the avoided tax collector. He welcomed the worship of the sinful woman and rescued the one caught in adultery. We could go on and on and on, but what we must realize is that the Jesus whom we read about in the Gospels is more like God than the one many of us picture in our minds, crossing his arms and shaking his head while we run around trying to get our lives together.

He is completely and 100 percent an exact replica of the Father. "Very truly I tell you, the Son can do nothing by himself; he can do only what he sees his Father doing, because whatever the Father does the Son also does. For the Father loves the Son and shows him all he does" (John 5:19–20). Jesus did what the Father showed him, which means that Jesus's heart was directly representative of the Father's heart.

Faithful Failures

I have an amazing friend, Sarah. Her heart is as big as they come. She is single, in her late 30s, and surrendered to full-time foster care. In fact, we all stood by and cheered as she recently adopted one of her first placements. Watching her love on her kids overwhelms my soul.

One of her hardest cases was a teenage foster daughter we will call D. Sarah's not very tall. In fact, both of my girls, who are 15 and 13, are already taller than Sarah. So it didn't take much for D to be bigger than Sarah. But she was also stronger, louder, and quite a bit more demanding than my friend. Despite several behavioral issues, Sarah got all the way in with parenting D.

Sarah put her whole self out there. She fought for D and always drove her to visits with her mom and grandma. She bought her clothes and school supplies and allowed her to experience a side of life she hadn't had the luxury of living.

In spite of Sarah's efforts, D seemed unable to receive Sarah's love. Parenting a child who has been so traumatized is extremely difficult. Sarah battled till the end because the longer D stayed with Sarah, the more strongly she resisted Sarah. At one point, D's resistance actually became dangerous and started to cause harm to Sarah, who had no choice but to surrender.

In the midst of Sarah's hard decision, the Midwest was hit with a huge ice storm. We woke up that January day to cancelled schools and work commute delays. The ground was a solid sheet of ice. In an effort to get to work on time, Sarah asked D to take Finn, their little Yorkie, outside to go to the bathroom. D refused in a verbally aggressive way.

There was some yelling exchanged, and D screamed profanity and got a little physical. Sarah shouted something ugly back and then walked outside, slammed the door, hit the first step covered in ice, and was instantly flat on her back, pain reeling throughout her entire body.

Hours later, Sarah was in the emergency room, unable to move. Sarah's fall had broken her back, and she would be laid up in bed for the next 12 weeks, unable to move or tend to her demands as a foster mom.

D had to be removed from the home since Sarah simply could not care for her in this condition. With the removal of D, my friend was instantly filled with shame and guilt. The image Sarah had in her head of the Father looked much like the one I already described—distant, disgruntled, standing far back, arms crossed, head shaking in disappointment. The story line running through her head replayed their dreadful morning over and over again, feeding her the lie that she did a bad job, that she was a bad foster mom.

We simply cannot afford to speak to ourselves in a way that God wouldn't speak to us. These words of condemnation were not God's, and he did not want credit for them. Lying in her bed, Sarah in her shame convinced herself to believe the lie that she had failed and that because of her failure, she was unable to move forward. Stuck in needing to re-earn God's affection and approval, she prepared to bring D back into her home, this time hoping things would end well.

"Who told you that you didn't end well?" I asked Sarah when she shared some of her shame with me. I looked at her and said something like this: "I am an imperfect parent at best, and if I watched my child lay their life down and try to do what you've done for the past year, the last thing I would be focused on is your hard ending. I would look at the love D has been shown, the family she's come to know, the worship songs she belts out from the back seat of your SUV, and the healthy rhythms she's been exposed to."

Then I added even more. "So what if you had a bad morning, yelled back, lost your cool, and then fell on the ice. So what if your time ended abruptly before you were able to fix yourself and your reaction to D. None of that disqualifies you. In fact, your shortcomings are actually what qualifies you. The Father isn't looking for you to do this perfectly. I don't think he's the least bit upset with you. I think he's honored that you would go to such great lengths to try to love one of his other children. I think he's bursting with pride."

The failures don't disqualify the faith. They actually enhance it. It's easy to have faith in something we know we can do. Sarah stepped into something she couldn't do. God's love for her didn't shift based on her inability to do perfectly what she set out to do. He already knew she couldn't do it to begin with. His love is steady, it's consistent, it's trustworthy, it's dependable.

James 1:17 (ESV) says, "Every good gift and every perfect gift is from above, coming down from the Father of lights, with whom there is no variation or shadow due to change." I love the second part of this verse, the part where it refers to God as something with no variation, no changing shadow. The reassurance James gives us is that no matter what happens around us, we can trust God to be steady, to stand strong, to stay faithful. He doesn't change based on what we do or don't do. He is who he is all the time.

When Sarah broke her back, it was not a punishment because she had failed. It wasn't the reaction of a disgruntled dad trying to punish her for getting it wrong. God didn't cause her back to break; he doesn't bring harm to course-correct. The ice caused her back to break, but in the midst of her broken back, God stayed present and worked. He was there inviting her to rewrite the story in the way of redemption.

If you feel misused or abused in your relationship with God, if you beat yourself up over side steps and shortcomings, if shame is your middle name, and if the story line on repeat in your head is a constant letdown, then you don't need more responsibility. You don't need to try harder to do better. You need more relationship—more of God. He doesn't need you to do more to prove you are worth more of him. He doesn't really need you to do anything. He is God, and his plan was never built around your perfection. It was actually built because of your imperfection.

Recognize the Lies

For so much of my life, I just wanted God to like me. I lived to make him proud. Always trying to get his attention, I never thought for a second that he genuinely wanted to just be near me. I never believed that he liked me, chose me, and invited me before I ever did a single thing to make me worthy. I lived for his approval and his affection, which left me experiencing many highs and lows, depending on the circumstances of any given day.

The enemy speaks lies of condemnation and shame into our heads that would make us see the Father's posture shifting in regard to our actions. That's exactly what he did to Adam and Eve. Satan takes the truth and twists it, causing us to doubt the strength of our relationship. But that's just not who God is. "The steadfast love of the LORD never ceases; his mercies never come to an end" (Lam. 3:22 ESV).

Our God is the perfect Father. He is unchanging, and his word never fails. His gentleness brings me near. His kindness leads to my repentance. He is not kind to me because of my repentance. He's kind to me because he loves me. Kind is who he is.

I don't know about you, but that's a God I want to be near. That's a God I want to always be present and working. Please hear me when I say this: God is for you. He loves you. He delights in you and wants to be near you. He's not keeping score. He's just here, always. His hand is out because he wants to be with you. Will you lower your inhibitions and come near?

CHAPTER EIGHT

God Waits for Me in My Realness

I am so grateful that God is both nearsighted and farsighted.
He sees us as we really are, and He sees how we'll really be.

—Beth Moore

She went to the well in the middle of the day for a reason. It was her way of avoiding, her attempt to escape. The looks, smirks, and remarks of the other women were just too much. She knew her life was a mess, but she didn't know what to do with the mess. Hard circumstances forced her into corner after corner, and it was fair to say that she did not navigate the tension well.

Scripture says, "Now he [Jesus] had to pass through Samaria" (John 4:4). This was an issue because Jews didn't go through Samaria. They avoided it at all costs. The Jews and the Samaritans didn't get along. Like most family feuds, how they got there is a long story for another day. You just need to know that these two groups of people had been enemies for generations.

Culture would say that Jesus didn't have to go through Samaria, but the Father had another idea. God knew a left turn into Samaria was necessary. There was a woman Jesus needed to meet there. She was avoiding her reality by dodging the fallen debris left on the ground through her broken choices. Look what happened when Jesus and the woman met.

> *When a Samaritan woman came to draw water, Jesus said to her, "Will you give me a drink?" (His disciples had gone into the town to buy food.) The Samaritan woman said to him, "You are a Jew and I am a Samaritan woman. How can you ask me for a drink?" (For Jews do not associate with Samaritans.) Jesus answered her, "If you knew the gift of God and who it is that asks you for a drink, you would have asked him and he would have given you living water."*
>
> *"Sir," the woman said, "you have nothing to draw with and the well is deep. Where can you get this living water? Are you greater than our father Jacob, who gave us the well and drank from it himself, as did also his sons and his livestock?" Jesus answered, "Everyone who drinks this water will be thirsty again, but whoever drinks the water I give them will never thirst. Indeed, the water I give them will become in them a spring of water welling up to eternal life."*
>
> —John 4:7–14

The woman goes on to ask Jesus if she can leave and go get her husband so he can also have some of this living water. She's thinking, *Great, no more midday well trips in an effort to avoid the other women. I can stop coming to the well all together.*

A clear sign of her thirst and the reality of her weariness is her quick attempt to further escape. Coming to the well day in and day out wasn't too much work; this was what the women did. It was their daily due diligence and how they best cared for their families. But coming to the well while avoiding the reality of all the emotions going on inside her heart had proved to be quite exhausting.

Jesus wasn't worried about the reality of this woman's life. Her mistakes weren't too much for him. He didn't care that she had been married four times or even that the man she was living with right then wasn't her husband. None of those things were too difficult for him. He wasn't going to tell her to get it together. He was inviting her to own it so he could get it together.

Jesus Reckons in Reality

Jesus waits for us in reality, in the real space of our actual hearts. The problem for many of us is that we don't live in reality. Aware or unaware, we tend to avoid reality when reality isn't what we thought it would be or how we planned it to be. We dodge hard emotions to get through our day, that meeting, or the family gathering. We're pretending to feel one way while we actually feel another way. We ignore triggers until we explode and leave in our path a wake of destruction because no matter how far we run, reality has a way of catching up with us.

Simon Tugwell, in his book *The Beatitudes*, wrote this:

> And so, like runaway slaves, we either flee our own reality or manufacture a false self, which is mostly admirable, mildly prepossessing, and superficially happy. We hide what we know or feel ourselves to be (which we assume to be unacceptable and unlovable) behind some kind of appearance which we hope will be more pleasing. We hide behind pretty faces which we put on for the benefit of our public. And in time we may even come to forget that we are hiding, and think that our assumed pretty face is what we really look like.[1]

Discipleship is not a fake-it-till-you-make-it training program. It's more of an own-it-till-you-grow-it trend. Jesus knew he had the answer to this woman's problems. I mean, in all realness, he was the answer to her problems. But he won't heal what we don't reveal, so he waited for her to be real. How you are really feeling is a great place of awareness. God is always present and always at work, but the place of his presence is in our reality and not in the places we pretend to be, hope to be, or some days flat out strive to be.

Today more than ever, we are equipped with the tools to avoid reality. To keep going or pushing ahead, all we need to do is grab our phones out of our back pockets. Gone are the days where we have to live in the uncomfortable of the real. Are you uneasy at the doctor's office? Just scroll through social media, and numb your mind with other people's problems. Are you disappointed with your spouse? Get in bed early, and binge-watch your favorite television drama to avoid acknowledging your feelings. Are you fearful of the future? Go ahead and create that list of everything you need to do to achieve, and live into the lie that once you get there, you will feel better.

The avoidance of our realness is one of the enemy's greatest war tactics. If he can keep us from being fully present right where we actually are, then he can also keep us from recognizing the God who is always working and always present in our realities.

I can be in one place, but my feelings may be in another place, all at the same time. Leaving me with a choice to make, do I pay attention to what I'm feeling, or do I push those feelings to the side and hope they go away? Do I acknowledge the tension and check my heart, or do I find something to distract me?

Grown-Up Feelings

I grew up in the days of silencing your feelings. If my feelings didn't work to my advantage, then they were in the way and needed to be dealt with promptly. I hushed them, beat them down, and got them in line—whatever it took to keep them from acting up. So many kids today grow up living their feelings. If you feel it, do it.

If it feels right to you, then it's right to me. Go with your heart. Do what you think is right.

Our feelings are not meant to be silenced and shamed, nor are they meant to be uplifted and praised. Rather, they are meant to be patiently parented. At the time of your salvation, you entered into the process of sanctification. You were justified by the cross (just as if you've never sinned.) That was immediate. Grace reached you, and forgiveness was issued. But your feelings in that moment were not magically transformed to look, act, and feel like Jesus. Your feelings began their process of sanctification. They started growing up.

We can't grow up feelings we never parent. Imagine our kids without any parents guiding them. Day in and day out, I interact with adults who have never acknowledged their feelings and therefore have never grown them up. On the outside, they may sound like Jesus, but on the inside, they feel far from Jesus. They fake it in hopes of one day making it. You were not created to just look and sound like Jesus; you were created to feel like Jesus.

What is on the inside eventually makes its way to the outside. We have all been on the receiving end of erupted feelings, that place where someone has held it in for so long, where they have faked it over and over again in hopes of making it, and then one thing slips, and the volcano blows. Out spews everything they've actually been feeling for months but never acknowledged.

Spiritual maturity is recognizing that your feelings are not the issue; they are the invitation—an invitation to do something with what you feel. Jesus wasn't worried about the many feelings the woman at the well was experiencing. He simply needed her to openly acknowledge her feelings because that place would be where she encountered him for healing.

Who Drives Your Car?

Think about it like this: feelings make really bad drivers. They don't know what they are doing or where they are going, and if they are allowed in the driver's seat for too long, they will inevitably end up in a ditch on the side of the road. Instead of handing your feelings the keys to the family minivan, try buckling those feeling into the passenger seat.

With our feelings buckled in, we then have the opportunity to drive them in the direction they need to go. We have the chance to parent them. Feelings will tell you a lot about who you are. They will help you see where you are well adjusted, rested, and equipped and where you are hurried, stressed, and over-anxious. Do you need control? Do you need answers? Are you patient, defensive, or forceful? Your feelings are really good informers of what's actually going on in the reality of your heart, and if you buckle them in, they might tell you all sorts of things.

The Truth behind Our Feelings

The place the Father wants to meet you is right in the middle of your feelings, because behind those feelings camps a lot of truth about your heart. Feelings are valuable for our formation. If you learn to partner with your feelings appropriately, they will show you things you wouldn't otherwise see.

Lysa TerKeurst wrote in her book *It's Not Supposed to Be This Way*:

> My feelings and my faith will almost certainly come into conflict with each other. My feelings see rotten situations as absolutely unnecessary hurt that stinks. My soul sees it as fertilizer for a better future. Both these perspectives are real. And they yank me in different directions with never-ending wrestling.[2]

When you feel something that doesn't look or sound like what you know of Jesus, the invitation is to figure out why. Think about it. You are an heir to the throne. Your dad owns the cattle on a thousand hills. He has promised you an inheritance and has given you the keys to his Kingdom. He has plans for you, hopes for you, dreams for you. He tells you not to worry about tomorrow, and every morning, he provides you with new mercies.

But sometimes, regardless of what your Father says, your feelings tell you to fret. They pull you into overthinking and play a highlight reel of worst-case-scenarios in your mind. You feel angry when you can't control things, threatened when someone does better than you, and isolated when you fail. You hide in depression, check out from the world, get lost in social media, and swallow your inner feelings of jealousy and unforgiveness. You do all that in an effort to not deal with what inconvenient feelings might be happening in your heart.

Here's the issue, though. God doesn't play pretend because he isn't put off by your feelings. You may move on, but he hangs tight. He knows you are in process. He understands how you grow. If you never have a place where you can be real with where you actually are, then you will never move forward.

God isn't put off by what you are putting off. He's patient enough to wait for you to stop and own the reality of the hard place you are currently living. The strength you need to move forward through your disappointing things is often on the other side of your real things. God refuses to enter into the place you pretend to be because the place where he is, is the place you need to be.

Round and Round

We have roundabouts on the roads all throughout my community. They are amazing if you know how to handle them. A long country road that used to have four stop signs now has four roundabouts. I don't have to stop but only go slow enough to make my way around the roundabout and then gently accelerate back to my desired speed. It really does make a difference—until an uninformed roundabout driver messes up the entire system.

There are people who think that instead of eliminating one stop, the roundabout actually added two to four. Instead of breezing through the circle, the driver actually stops at each entry point, makes sure the approaching cars are going to wait, and then merge accordingly. It's maddening because the system makes sense when it is used properly but doesn't when it is misused. It actually does the opposite of what it is intended to do.

Remember back in the beginning of this book when we talked about the Hebrews and their panicked pursuit of freedom? Instead of standing in confidence, they cowered in fear. They did the same thing again in the desert when they start grumbling for meat to eat instead of the manna God had provided. And again, when Moses went up on the mountain for an extended period of time, the people grew tired of waiting obediently and decided to melt their gold and create idols they could worship. And think about the time they were invited into an encounter with the one true God and instead opted to send Moses in their place.

We could keep going because the whole thing is one big feeling fiasco meant for their forming but instead forcing their ending. Jeff Manion, in *The Land Between*, writes about their desert journey: "The desert is not intended to be their final destination but rather a necessary middle space where they will be formed as a people and established in their connection to God."[3]

It was only meant to be an alley they passed through, a shadow of insecurity they wrestled with. Their invitation all along was to the place of freedom, the place where they would no longer be shaped by what happened outside of them because they learned to give way to the shape taking over inside of them. But they couldn't do it. They couldn't take the keys away from their feelings, and ultimately their feelings drove them right over the cliff to their finish. They missed everything because they refused to acknowledge how they were feeling.

When Unraveling Is Unnerving

My left turn brought with it a lot of change. Dave and I sensed it coming, and we did our best to prepare our girls. But to go from a mega church with close to 6,000 people in weekly attendance, four services, a family fun bookstore, a cafeteria, and amazing dollar nachos to a broken-down, powerless, dangerous, dirty, grim firehouse left our kids struggling just a bit. Their entire worlds seemed to be flipped upside down. One minute they were attending four weekend services with all the bells and whistles, and the next they were being told not to pick up any needles they may see laying in the grass next door.

At this point, I had adjusted to the unknown of my reality, but as a mom, watching my girls deal with their hard feelings in the midst of the turn became increasingly difficult. They didn't ask to be there; they weren't given an option. Forced to follow by default, the turn felt somewhat calloused and even cruel.

Our girls said goodbye so bravely as we ended our time at the church. They collected messages and phone numbers from all their favorite teachers and friends, hugged hundreds of confused people who often comforted them through what didn't make sense, and then they bravely followed us out the door.

They asked me hard questions. Why would they let Dad go? He was the best children's pastor ever. Why didn't God step in and stop this? Where are we going to go next? Who are we going to be if we aren't the pastor's kids?

I did my best to answer their questions honestly, but most of the time I found myself just saying "I don't know." The truth was, I didn't know. None of it made sense to me either, but it still felt like God knew what he was doing. Most of the time, I kept it together in front of the girls. I was honest to the point that I thought they could handle it, and then when we reached that point, I would put on my brave I'm-not-worried face, and we would keep going.

I had, however, stopped pretending with God. He didn't get my put-together answer. He got the full frontal fear of a momma tired from watching her kids push through something they didn't ask for. They had done so well. They were completely out of their element at Hose House #4, and yet they were going for it. It's one thing for God to invite me to turn left and give me more than I can handle, but for him to do it to my kids. . . . I didn't know if they could handle the hardships in front of them. I didn't know if they had the faith to navigate the unknown gap we found ourselves in. Did they trust me? Did they trust God?

A Little Bit of Hope in a Whole Lot of Jewelry

One afternoon, Ella asked me if she could help raise money for the Hose House. Impressed by her enthusiasm, I started talking to her about the things she loved to do and how they might benefit the place where we were. In the end, we developed a bracelet-making plan. Ella decided to buy some beads, and string them together into bracelets, sell them, and then give all the money to the Hose House. She decided she would call her bracelet company Hope Jewelry.

For the next several months, my girls made bracelets like nobody's business, and everywhere we went, we sold Hope Jewelry, matching T-shirts, and business cards. Ella is a much better business owner than I am. She was always prepped and prepared, beautifully presenting her goods for everyone to see.

If I were guest speaking at a church or retreat, Ella and her jewelry went with me. If we were at the Hose House, Ella had a table set up with her jewelry. The rule was to sell it to people visiting but give it freely to the people in the community. She did a great job! Who doesn't want to buy a beaded bracelet from a little girl raising money to take care of her community? She outsold my books 10 to 1 everywhere we went (not that I am bitter about her minutes of work versus my hours). I was simply grateful for a glimmer of light in the sudden transition.

One day while we were driving to the Hose House, Ella looked at me and said, "Mom, I think I want a store for my jewelry." I laughed out loud at her lack of reality and said, "Ella, babe, your dad and I don't have jobs right now. The last thing we can do is get you a store for your jewelry. Maybe someday, okay? For now, let's just keep doing what we are doing."

Our conversation ended there, and I'm sure neither of us thought another thing about it—until the next day. I dropped Ella off at school early that morning and went back home. I checked my email a few hours later to find a message from someone I didn't know. She told me her story of how she and a friend just opened a store in Hamilton called Made to Love. Their store sold goods made in Haiti to raise money for the education of the Haitian kids. But since they were located in Hamilton, they were sensing the pull to partner with local missions, and they had heard that my daughter made bracelets to raise money for the Hose House. They were reaching out to see if she would possibly be interested in putting her bracelets in their store to help her sales and their mission.

I almost signed Ella out of school early. I couldn't believe it! She didn't even pray about it. There's no way she told the Father about wanting that store. But she was real with me on what her heart wanted. She owned her desires. She owned her reality, and when she said it out loud that day in our car, the always-working and ever-present God heard it, and within hours, she had herself a store. I was blown away.

God knows the desires of our hearts, but he also waits for us to own them. He is faithful to meet us right where we are, but he is also dedicated to waiting for us to really be there. God knew I was struggling with trusting him to work this left turn out for the good of my girls, and in my struggle, he met me there and became my strength.

Letting Go of What Didn't Happen

I don't think we mean to hide from God. The woman at the well didn't set out to avoid the Messiah, but in disregarding her reality, it's what she did. Anytime we press down bitterness, deny pain or misunderstanding, silence judgment, or dismiss anger in an effort to just get in line and do the right thing, we unconsciously begin to operate in an alternate reality. We are no longer really being real.

Instead, we are wrapped up in a false version of ourselves because who has time to deal with all those feelings?

All the while God waits for us to turn left in authenticity. "God, I'm feeling this. It doesn't feel like Jesus, but I believe if I bring it to the light, you will help me to see where it's coming from." In that place of realness, we find the open arms of a Father who has been waiting for us.

The gospel is about living life in freedom. I do not have to be governed or dictated by my latest and greatest feelings. I can have them, but they can't have me. In order for any of this to take place, we have to learn to be people who reckon with reality. We have to stop putting on masks, posting fake profile pics, or hiding behind savvy one-liners. We must allow our walls to come down and learn to embrace the reality of our unraveling. You are where you are, so be there all the way.

My unraveling was important because when I could no longer keep myself intact, I found the one who holds all things together. For a lot of my life, I've been told I was *too much*. Sometimes, it was that I worked too hard. Other times, I was too hard on myself, too over-the-top about Jesus, too expressive on stage when I taught. At some point, all the too-muches caused me to shrink back and hide. I softened myself, my drive, my passion, and my feelings so other people didn't feel uncomfortable. In doing so, I also softened my connection to the Father. You know who I will never be too much for? The God who created me.

Some of you have dealt with other lies, that instead of being too much, *you are never enough*. You're quiet, reserved, timid, disengaged. But whatever the label is doesn't matter. What matters is that these are all descriptors of real feelings, and if we don't bring them in front of Jesus, we will never be refined to become who he created us to be.

There were moments after my left turn that my mind got the best of me. I took the keys to my car and drove down unpaved, dirty roads. I wondered what would have happened if I hadn't quit my job. What if I had just taken the position they offered?

The what-ifs of life can also not be reality. The only road I could walk down was the road I was actually on. Spending any amount of energy on the unpaved road of our lives would be wasted energy—energy I didn't have as I climbed this hill.

God doesn't hang out in false realities because He's not afraid of the reality of your reality. He's not worried about what you should have done, what you wish you *would have* said or how the other person *could have* responded. It's one thing to learn something from what did or didn't happen, but it's an entirely different thing to live in that imaginary place, replaying it over and over again, wishing for a different outcome. Shaming, name blaming, trying to make sense of your feelings—they will never work. Your feelings must be brought to your Savior.

I can't avoid myself and move toward God at the same time. He waits with the real me, not the me I keep putting off. He is not waiting for a future, better, prettier, smarter, more controlled me. He is simply waiting for all of me. I will not get where I am going unless I first acknowledge and deal with where I currently am. And so He waits for me there because He cares more about me as a person than where I'm headed.

It's the same invitation for you. Will you come fully into God's presence and just be where you are? Just be tired, angry, bitter, broken, fearful, discouraged, tempted, excited. Just be real because that's who he wants to encounter. That's who he wants to heal. That's who he longs to help. This place of realness and rawness will become the place of your transformation.

> *Come to me, all you who are weary and burdened, and I will give you rest. Take my yoke upon you and learn from me, for I am gentle and humble in heart, and you will find rest for your souls. For my yoke is easy and my burden is light.*
>
> —Matt. 11:28–30

Jesus isn't offering rest to those who pretend to have it all together. He offers it to the real, the hurting, the broken. It's what he offered to the woman at the well, the rich young ruler, and the man lying on his mat by the pool of Bethesda, and it's what he's offering to you. Own up to why you are where you are. Be real with yourself and those around you. Don't delay or deny. Look deep inside at what's happening under the surface. Let Jesus in there. If you want to live in the full freedom of what you have been promised, you have to live in the fully exposed reality of where you currently exist. And I promise, over time, reality just isn't that bad.

CHAPTER NINE

God Cares More Than I Do

God is not after great performances or great movements.
He is after us!

—Jennie Allen

I am competitive by nature and hate to lose, so the pressure of perfection didn't overpower me as much as it possessed me. It was a double-edged sword. When I knew I could do what I set out to do, I did it, and I did it well. But when my achievement was up in the air, I hesitated to get to work, wondering if my faith would be able to withstand my potential failure.

On the highway of my faith, I found safety in numbers. Surrounded by people all the time almost made failure nonexistent because I could step out and excel when I knew I would hit the ball out of the park and shy back and let someone else take the lead when a foul might be likely. Looking back, there were countless promptings I ignored because they lacked the guarantee of success.

Turning left meant climbing a hill I hadn't conquered yet. It showed signs of debris and danger. It was definitely out of my comfort zone. It meant learning that my future wasn't dependent on not failing and that, in fact, my future was and is solidified because of my failures.

Following Jesus to this new place forced me to step into the shadow of failure. I didn't know where we were going, let alone how we would get there. I wasn't good at navigating the unknown and unexpected. When Paul says we must run the race to win the prize (1 Cor. 9:24), he is talking about winning, but he's not talking about winning the way we envision winning. Victory, thank God, is not dependent on our lung capacity. We don't run to win; we run because Jesus has already won. The prize is Jesus; it's being with him in the midst of our participation.

I had yet to realize I was running as though winning was up to me. Climbing this new hill with the weight of disappointment and future disillusionment, I struggled to put one foot in front of the next. I had no choice but to slow down. With a change of pace, I began noticing something about myself. I struggled to not be the best, and my drive for perfection left me working myself silly. I ran with massive amounts of pressure on my shoulders, and the extra weight was going to keep me from climbing the hill in front of me.

Exhausted from the tension of turning left and walking away from my job, I dealt with what it felt like to not make the team. The truth is, I wanted to stay, but what the Father told me was next for my life wasn't a possibility for me. He made it clear it was time for me to go. The only way to overcome the fear of rejection is to be rejected and live through it. It was the first time in my adult life that I can remember really wanting something while at the same time that something wanted something else.

The Lie That Is Fear

Fear is crippling. Imagine our kids learning how to walk while they're overwhelmed with a fear of falling. It would paralyze their chances to learn something they were created to do. They would cower with every small step, overcalculating their next decision, hesitating with each sway. Even after they knew they could do it, they would count the cost, checking to see if their possible misstep was worth walking to go get the toy. They would always be aware of who was watching because failing in front of other people takes it to another level.

I don't know about you, but when my girls took their first steps I acted like a crazy person. I told everyone. I took videos and plastered them all over social media. Their steps were clumsy and awkward, they wobbled and fell again and again, but I went nuts cheering for them. I was their biggest fan, and not for a second was I focused on their falling. Each time they went down, I ran to them, picked them up, put them back on their feet, brushed off any dirt, and invited them to try again.

If we celebrate the strengths of our kids even in the midst of their failures, imagine how much more our perfect Father in heaven does the same for us. Before I turned left, I deemed him a Father who needed me to get it right. The pressure I put on myself was because I wanted my achievements to make him proud. I didn't want him standing off in the distance, shaking his head in disappointment.

I've walked with my kids through some pretty tough failures and rejections, and what I've experienced in the midst of the hard realities is an opportunity to grow closer, band together, and come away stronger. The time of failure actually becomes the time of forward movement. It's beautiful! Don't get me wrong, I love my kids' strengths and love watching them win, but their failures provide me with an opportunity that their successes don't. In their weaknesses, they need me, and in that place, we strengthen our connection.

It's Not All on You

Because God cares more about it than you do, the pressure isn't all on you. I was on the phone the other day with a friend of a friend. She was going through a really hard time with her marriage, family, and the general direction of her life. As I listened, she told me the details of why she had been stuck for years in this place of not knowing what to do. The one thing that stood out the most to me was her fear. She was afraid to move because she didn't want to mess up God's plan.

Her questions were real. What if she got it wrong? What if her choices left someone she cared about out of reach for Jesus's redemption? What if what she did caused another person to never move forward, thus robbing them of the path God had for them in their life? What if she messed everything up?

I listened for about 30 minutes until I gently began to compare the God she knew, this harsh God who turns his head and distances himself from us when we don't tow the line perfectly, to the God I was coming to know. I recognized my old self in so many of her thoughts—not all of them, but enough to resonate with the pressure she put on herself to make the right choices. That same pressure had once crippled me, rendering me useless. But not anymore.

Off the beaten path, I realized that God actually cares more about it than I do. He does. That thing you are worried about—he cares about it more. That thing you are losing sleep over—he cares about it more. Your marriage, your kids, your finances, your future, anything you care about—God cares about them more.

It's actually impossible for you to out-care God. He created caring. And his kindness led him to create a system that doesn't fail even when we do. I don't have to win every race because God already did that. He crossed the finish line, won the relay, and received the ribbon. The victory is already mine; I simply get to participate.

Go ahead and insert all the jokes about participation trophies here. Big surprise! I am not a fan of them in real life. Nothing is better than working your way to the top in a soccer tournament and leaning forward so they can slide that first place medal around your neck. It's such a fun accomplishment. But when it comes to participation trophies in the Kingdom, I am all for it. The Father is a much better reward, and we can be with him and experience more of heaven on earth—the fullness of the Kingdom right here and right now. That's the prize. That's why we run, and God is what we win. The more we run, the more we participate, and the more fully we experience all God has for us this side of heaven.

And here's the best part. None of it is about us getting it right. My friend didn't have to sit, unmoving, crippled by the fear of getting it wrong year after year. She just needed to get moving and run the race Jesus was inviting her to run, even if she didn't do it perfectly.

A god who needs us to get everything right isn't very godly. But God is the Creator of the universe. He spins the world like a basketball on top of his index finger. He did not base the entire well-being of the planet on our getting it right every single time. He put a plan in place for our redemption and restoration and invited us into his fail-proof system that's not about our rightness but about his righteousness.

The Daunting Task of Doing Nothing

My left turn put me on a hill full of debris and construction equipment. Physically, I had to slow down, readjust my focus, and change my breathing. Making it to the top depended on these adjustments. Following Jesus off the beaten path in discipleship can feel like just another hill to climb. Those of us who are high achievers will be tempted to add it to our to-do list for the sheer thrill of checking it off once we finish.

I don't mind a good competition, but this is not that. This is not just another hill to climb, race to win, or trophy to display. If your left turn has left you with a list of things you now need to do, then fold up your list and tuck it away because thinking this is about what we will do will limit our exposure to all God has done. My time spent doing nothing taught me that God did everything.

I got my girls off to school, poured my second cup of coffee, and sat down in the big comfy chair by the window in our bedroom. It was week one of being at home, and I was determined to make the most of my time. I pulled out my journal, felt-tip pens, Bible, and the Bible study I was working through. I had grand visions dancing around my mind of book-writing, blog-posting, and platform-building. As I opened my journal, I asked the Father what he wanted me to do now that I had quit my job. "Where do we start, Lord? What is it you want me to do?"

"Nothing." I must have heard him incorrectly. Surely he didn't want me to do nothing. I just turned left, gave up my job, and started down this unknown road to write my first book. This was not the time to sit back and do nothing. I pressed in and asked him again, "What do you want me to do?"

"This isn't about what you are doing, I want you to do nothing."

"Okay I hear what you are saying, Lord. How do you want me to go about doing nothing?" I was still hoping to put together some sort of a checklist. I simply did not know how to do nothing. I am the person who does something.

In order for me to clearly see God's work in my life, my work had to cease. I did not do nothing well, but thankfully, there were two girls in my house who appeared to be experts. My girls knew how to do nothing and not feel guilty. They knew how to spend hours coloring, watching television, and playing Mario Kart or Just Dance, never feeling one ounce of guilt or shame. They never worried that they had other things they should be doing or that they were missing out on something important. They didn't shame themselves for wasting time.

In fact, they never shamed themselves for inviting me in on their nothings.

"Mom, color with me."

"Mom, watch this show with me."

"Mom, play Just Dance again."

They did what I would have called nothing all the time, and they made it look so easy.

That being said, guess what I did? I let my kids become the teachers. I watched their play, their freedom, and their fun. That season, Ella and I colored like our lives depended on it. We filled up adult coloring books as though they were going to disappear. Addy and I watched all kinds of movies. We played video games. Actually, we achieved top status on Super Mario Brothers.

Now before you start thinking this was easy, you need to know that my mind did not call this play productive. I was very much a Martha in a Mary moment. I filled my schedule with things I loved doing—things I had given up for the sake of being productive. I played soccer at the local indoor facility a couple nights a week, watched movies in the middle of the day, and just hung out with friends for no reason other than to be together.

Doing nothing had honestly never been so exhausting.

One morning I found a note tucked under my coffee pot. It was from Addy. She is my encourager, always leaving sweet things around the house for me to find. Her note this morning struck a deep chord with me. Her little note, in the sweetest, partially illegible handwriting said, "Mom, thank you for working so hard for Ella and me. We don't know what we would do without you. We love you. Addy."

In my season of doing nothing, Addy considered it everything. It was everything to her because my time had been spent in her presence. Her measurement of my productivity wasn't how many sermons I preached or how many pages I wrote. She didn't care about my job title, description, or accomplishments. She simply basked in my presence. It was about being together.

If my daughter finds that much enjoyment in my presence, imagine how my heavenly Father feels when he is with me. He delights in my presence. As I rest in him, he actually works for me.

I am writing this chapter sitting in the waiting room at the hospital. Yesterday my grandpa, who has been hospitalized for about two weeks, had some major complications and was rushed into emergency surgery. I was out of town when my mom called. I had planned for a two-day-away writing stint so I could make some major progress on this book you're reading right now.

I had literally just sat down to start writing when my phone rang. The panic in Mom's voice had me up and packing before she even got her words out. It suddenly didn't matter what I had planned. I just needed to be with my grandpa. I rushed to the hospital, trying to stay focused on the road through the tears blurring my eyes.

Not once did I think about working. Not once did I worry about what I wasn't getting done. I did nothing but be present. At the end of this long day, I buckled myself into my car, turned on my heated seat, and opened my email before starting my drive home. Wouldn't you know, there was an email from a publishing magazine letting me know that my first book, *Bigger: Rebuilding the Broken*, had been chosen as one of their feature books, and they planned to run it as an upcoming feature in their monthly magazine. I literally laughed out loud. I hadn't done anything, and in the midst of my nothing, God did everything.

We can always trust him to be working for us because he actually cares about it more than we do. He does. This was his idea. He put these dreams in my heart. He inspired me to pursue a life of ministry, teaching, writing, and discipleship. This was all his idea, and he actually cares about it more than I do. He cares about *it* more, and he cares about *me* more. As a parent, I will not sit idly back while my kids work, plan, and pray for their futures. I will step in and do what I can to assist. They will walk through doors I can open because, if I am able, I will open them. Why would I do that? Because I care about *it*—and I can about *them*—more.

I care about their futures more than they do, not in a way that will leave me forcing them to work harder and do better or in a way that will enable them to not work, but in a way that will invite them to rest well. They can work from a place of rest because they are in good hands, and together we make a better team.

Learning to Be Childlike

One of the most essential pieces of your faith is to become childlike in your interactions with God. I know you have worked hard to grow up. You value responsibility, and the people around you benefit from your advancement. But the most profitable thing you will ever do is learn to be responsibly dependent on your Father. On this journey, the way to follow is to trust, and the way to trust is like childhood attachment.

There's something the Father wants to show you, something he has for you, something he wants to give you. His gift is not based on what you do. Your achievements won't release it. Actually, it comes in the midst of your rest when you lay everything aside and pull in close to your Father.

> *The LORD is the everlasting God, the Creator of the ends of the earth. He will not grow tired or weary, and his understanding no one can fathom. He gives strength to the weary and increases the power of the weak. Even youths grow tired and weary, and young men stumble and fall; but those who hope in the LORD will renew their strength. They will soar on wings like eagles; they will run and not grow weary, they will walk and not be faint.*
> —Isa. 40:28–31

We don't learn how strong God is and how much he cares if we never stop long enough to press in while he presses on.

I don't know where you need his strength, but I am confident that something is coming to your mind as you read this. What might it look like for you to rest in him? Is there something for you to do, somewhere for you to go, someone for you to call? Or are you more like me and hear this as an invitation into nothing? Who knows? Your nothing might actually turn you left toward his everything.

The disciples left their lives behind, turned left, and followed Jesus off the beaten path. They didn't know where they were going or how they were going to get there. They didn't have the skills, the tools, or the experience to do what was in front of them. It's a good thing their journey wasn't about their résumé. They didn't have to know the way; they journeyed with the way. Jesus was their true north. His connection with the Father provided the compass necessary to advance the Kingdom forward. The disciples didn't have to worry. Jesus was connected and cared more about their journey than they did.

CHAPTER TEN

God Is about the Yes Way More Than the No

God has hidden mighty and mysterious things for us,
not from us.

—Bill Johnson

From Drowning to Door-Opening

I will teach about turning left until the day I die because it holds so much weight for me. Jesus and his disciples turned left. They stepped off the beaten path and set out to do what no one else had done before. Each time the crowds gathered, Jesus seemed unmoved by them. What they needed he always seemed to have, but he never forced his way in.

By this point in the journey, the disciples caught on to the supernatural side of Jesus. He was connected in an abundant way. Nothing was off limits. There always seemed to be a yes available to him.

Take the feeding of the 5,000. The disciples failed to see the yes present with just a simple basket of fish and a few loaves of bread before them. They thought they needed to send the hungry people home because they lacked the necessary nutrients to fill their bellies. But Jesus knew the bread in the basket was a piece of his miracle. He took what the disciples saw as the no and blessed it, and before their eyes it became a yes.

Following that miracle of multiplication, Jesus put his guys in a boat and sent them across the sea. He planned to catch up with them later. Out on the water, in the middle of the night, the disciples saw what looked like a ghost walking toward them. I don't know who it was that first realized the silhouette they saw was Jesus, but Simon Peter was the first to notice his invitation.

> "LORD, if it's you," Peter replied, "tell me to come to you on the water."
> "Come," he said.
> Then Peter got down out of the boat, walked on the water and came toward Jesus.
> —Matt. 14:28–29

Peter saw the yes. If Jesus was present, Peter was invited. He didn't need to do anything first. There was no class he needed to take or forum he needed to consult. He didn't need to perform any rituals. He simply needed to take a step forward in obedience. Jesus said, "Come."

Here's what Peter didn't think about in the moment. He didn't think about the sacrifice. In the few seconds before his feet touched the cold, dark water, he didn't make a list of how this could go wrong and what it might cost him. He simply stepped out of the boat and went to meet his teacher.

I meet so many people who think discipleship is just about saying no to dozens of things so they can say yes to God. Initially, they have a point. We do have to say no, and our no will leave us laying things down. But this entire journey is built around God's yes to us. God the Father chose us, he said yes to us, and he will never stop saying yes to us.

God knows what we don't, and because of his infinite knowledge, he will often lead us with redirection. Picture a toddler determined to climb up and down the basement steps and the concerned parents who understand the basement steps are not the best place to learn this necessary skill. The parents' understanding leads them to redirect the curious child to a better yes. Walking in step with the Father is about learning to release our no and trust in his yes.

The disciples had to release what they expected their lives to look like in order to turn left. They said goodbye to their families and set out to follow Jesus off the beaten path. Every yes they said to him required a no to someone or something else, but the way they faced became the way they embraced, and as they walked, they grew in their ability to keep in step.

Son, Servant, or Slave

Saying yes as a child of God is different from saying yes as a servant or slave. A child says yes because they trust the invitation of their father. A servant or slave says yes because they must. Saying yes is their obligation.

Contrast that to the way you live in the Kingdom of God. He's invited you in, given you the keys to his home, and promised that you will be taken care of—they're all yes in my book. We then can either take our keys and use them to access all he's invited us into or pridefully put them in our pocket and continue to try to earn something we've actually already been given.

It's really the story of the prodigal. There were two brothers. The younger brother chose to leave his father's home, take his inheritance, and set out to find himself. The other brother stayed close to home and served his father well. The younger brother squandered all his money, ended up in a literal pigsty, and actually considered eating the slop he was feeding his master's pigs. Then he came to his senses and decided to go back home and ask Dad to graciously bring him back into his establishment, even just as hired help.

As the younger brother journeyed home, he rehearsed his apology in his head over and over. The closer he got to home, the more his body shook. To say he was nervous would be an understatement. His dad could say no, and then what would he do? Where would he go? But then he saw something. From afar he saw a figure running toward him. It looked like his father, but that couldn't be. Grown men of his stature do not run. It was unbecoming.

As the blur started to come into focus, he realized that it was his father. He was running, arms open, eyes watering. His father was happy to see him. His son coming back home wasn't a burden; he was a blessing—even after all he had done. Dad didn't even let him get a word out. Before the son's rehearsed apology made its way into the air, his father had put a robe around him and was ushering him into the house to prepare for the celebration. What was lost had now been found. What was blind could now see. What felt dead found new life.

Outside the house, the older brother looked up from his work in disbelief. How could his father betray him so after all he had done for dear old Dad? He never left him, never forsook him, and never stopped working. All the while, his little brother was out making a mockery of the entire family. What would possess his father to just welcome little brother back like he had truly changed? His brother obviously needed to pay for his sins.

It took me awhile to invite Jesus to be Lord of my life, but once I did, he had everything, and I never looked back. From the moment

I surrendered, my life was service. I spent more hours at church than the people who actually worked there. I straightened chairs, cleaned bathrooms, and picked up trash. I ran snack bars and led small groups. I was the only volunteer dumb (or young) enough to stay awake through the whole overnighter. You name it, I did it.

It's a slow, subtle shift in posture, but at some point, if we do not stay aware, we shift from a posture of serving as a son or daughter to a posture of serving as a slave or servant.

Later that night, Dad went outside to check on his older son. He hadn't made his way into the party to celebrate, and Dad wanted to make sure his eldest knew there was a seat at the table with his name on it. The older son said this to his father:

> *"Look! All these years I've been slaving for you and never disobeyed your orders. Yet you never gave me even a young goat so I could celebrate with my friends. But when this son of yours who has squandered your property with prostitutes comes home, you kill the fattened calf for him!"*

> *"My son," the father said, "you are always with me, and everything I have is yours. But we had to celebrate and be glad, because this brother of yours was dead and is alive again; he was lost and is found."*

> —Luke 15:29–32

The older brother refused his father's yes because he was offended by his brother's yes, and consequently, he missed out on the party. He made himself such a slave that he missed out on being a son.

Here's what you have to know. We can be either son in the story. We can be the wayward son out sowing our wild oats and living in rebellion or we can be the rigid, older son sticking close to home, doing the work and getting the job done. Proximity is not the primary focus; posture is. The younger brother came home, allowed himself to be received fully by his father's yes. He didn't deny the extravagant welcome-back party and humbly accepted his invitation into the fullness of his father's grace, mercy, and love. He decided to live from this place of love rather than for all the love he couldn't find out in the world.

The older brother stayed outside with his head down, working his hardest to earn his keep. He dug in and didn't dare take advantage of the wealth of his father, knowing that one day, if he did all the right things, he would be ushered in.

The father handed them both keys that day. To his youngest, the one he ran out to embrace, he handed a key to the kingdom and said something like this: "Yes, son, you are invited back in to all I have. Welcome home!" Then he stepped out of the party to bring in his oldest son. Maybe he said something like this: "All I've had all this time has been available to you. I don't have to give you the keys to my kingdom; they have always been in your pocket. You've had access to this throughout your entire life. Please come inside."

These were both the same invitation. One received it, and we actually don't know what happened to the other one. Jesus stopped telling the story as if to say, "So what are *you* going to do?"

Everyone who would have been listening to Jesus teach in that moment would have known that he was talking to the religious leaders and the Pharisees. They were the older brothers, the ones who had the keys to the Kingdom in their pockets the entire time and yet refused to humble themselves and come to the table to celebrate that the Father had invited everyone to the party.

If you've fully surrendered your life to Jesus, then you, too, have the keys to the Kingdom in your pocket. He's given you full access to all he has. You are invited into every single room. Jesus told his disciples, "If you remain in me and my words remain in you, ask whatever you wish, and it will be done for you" (John 15:7).

Remain in him—whatever they asked for would be given freely. The key was the word *remain* (*attach* or *abide* in some Bible versions).

The word is used close to six times in the first seven verses of John 15, which makes me think that Jesus really wants his guys to understand this. It's important that they know they have all they need when their lives are centered (remain) in his love.

What You See Is What You Be

Gospel eyes are about attachment. When we are centered and postured in a place of perfect love, we can pivot ourselves from this place freely, knowing that we have all we need and that what we don't have we don't need. We are children of a really good Father who is bent on providing for us. The direction we look will determine the way we go, and the way we go will determine the way we grow. If you want what God has for you, then look directly at where he has you, face it, and follow it.

I've been honest about my struggle to walk away from the mega church I called home and embrace the Hose House. I didn't see this part coming. I never asked for it, dreamed of it, or imagined it, and yet there I was, directly in the middle of it. The temptation was to look longingly at all I left behind, to replay how things could have gone differently, or to wish they were still the same. I could focus on the no and keep my eyes longingly on what I left behind, or I could shift my vision to the yes and awkwardly embrace this new terrain.

I remember wishing only part of my life could change. How nice it would be if some things just stayed the same. I held onto them, hoping I could turn the page and take them with me, but as long as I held onto them, I seemed to go nowhere. God was inviting me to something exciting, but my inability to fully embrace it kept me lingering in the distance.

By this point on the journey, I really liked the Hose House, and I loved the outside-of-the-box ministry we were experiencing. It was like nothing I had done before. My family was different there. That place was a good place. It was a restoring place. It was a necessary place. It just wasn't a pictured place.

Trying to turn left while walking backward and looking at all you are leaving behind is the movement of a misinformed servant or slave. Sons and daughters see the yes. They recognize the invitation to turn left with freedom and favor. They are able to receive fully the inheritance laid out before them. I knew in my head that God had so many things for my family and me, and turning left was my opportunity to live out this belief. Here's the question I had to answer: Could I let go of what was and embrace what I didn't know would come to be?

At some point in our journey, our relationship with Jesus will lead us off the beaten path. He will invite us away from what we know and more deeply into him. Saying no—turning away—will be hard. It will feel costly and maybe confusing, but it will also be holy. This is the road where trust is forged and friendship is built. This is the place we discover our yes.

Growing Old while Staying Young

I didn't have kids so I could employ them. In fact, if I did, I want my money back because they are not the best hired help. I can't tell you how many times I secretly reload the dishwasher because I know I can fit at least four more cups (don't tell anyone, but I do that with my mother-in-law, too.) My kids work as part of our family, but to do work is not why I had them.

Dave and I decided to have kids because we wanted to grow our family. We wanted to invest our lives and give away our love. Likewise, God is a Father in pursuit of sons and daughters. He's invited you into enjoyment, not employment. He didn't put Adam and Eve in the garden because he wanted to be a taskmaster. He wanted to be a dad.

Relationship breeds responsibility, and as sons and daughters, we will work and build and do things that will profit the family. But those things are meant to come from who we are rather than determine who we are.

When we see ourselves as sons or daughters, accepting the invitation of our very good Father, we stop flattering or fixing ourselves before responding with a yes, and we just respond. The more I looked at the yes God had for me, the clearer it became and the more beauty I saw.

We had been at the Hose House for about six or seven months, finally getting the hang of it when Ella told me she wanted to get baptized. The conversation sort of came out of left field. We hadn't been in a traditional church for quite some time now, but she insisted this was the time.

"That's great, Ella. Where do you want to get baptized?" I asked, thinking she might say her friend's church where she sometimes went on weekends.

"I want to get baptized at the Hose House," she answered without one ounce of hesitation.

I laughed at the irony of it all. A firehouse without water was a funny thing. The entire idea behind a firehouse is creating a system in which we can quickly get water onto fires and prevent damage. If we were going to have a baptismal service, we were going to need water. We picked a Sunday, scheduled the service, borrowed a baptismal from a friend's church, and extended the invitation to everyone in our community. Then we invited all our close friends and family and called the fire department down the road. Surely, they would help get the water we needed.

The morning of the baptism, Dave, the girls, and I got to the Hose House extra early to meet the Hamilton Fire Department. They sent over a truck, hooked their hose up to the nearby hydrant, and filled our baptismal to the top. The water was cold and a little murkier than those nice, warm baptismal tubs inside churches, but it would do the job perfectly. Our friends and families arrived, we worshiped, and then we invited everyone to gather in close. We baptized eight people that day, including both my girls.

As we finished with a worship song, I looked around the small, dirty building and felt so full. I always knew my girls would get baptized, but this wasn't how I had envisioned it. I assumed it would be inside our large church building in front of a loud crowd with the worship team playing, the camera recording, and the lights flashing.

Instead, it was quiet. Some were crying, all were close, and I was humbled. It wasn't what I thought it would be, but it was exactly as I knew it should be. God knows what he is doing. And even when we don't understand the yes and struggle with the no, we can trust and obey.

God has invited you as a son or daughter. As his child, you have the keys to the Kingdom. Turning left isn't about what you will say no to; it's about all he's said yes to on your behalf. For every loss, he has a win. For every wrong, he has a right. For every problem, he has a promise. For every issue, he has an invitation. Can you fully receive his yes today? Can you lay down your need to understand? Can you determine not to be threatened by the yes he has for someone else in your community? Can you redirect your eyes to the gospel invitation for your life? Can you trust that he's inviting you into something you want to be part of? Can you just say yes and turn and receive the fullness of all he's offered?

CHAPTER ELEVEN

God Is after My Heart, Not My Behavior

God is not concerned with accomplishing tasks.
God is interested in revealing Himself. This requires us to be
available. Some people, like Cain, insist that God must accept
what we offer Him. However, what God values most
is our obedience.

—Henry T. Blackaby

As I look back over my life, I know I've occasionally missed God's yes due to being too fixated on my no, but I am so thankful for the times I have been able to experience his goodness. Over and over, he has invited me to follow. Each time I have accepted his invitation, I've come away with more than I've left behind.

The Hose House was a big yes for me and my family. That chapter in my life is one I will always hold very near and dear. While we were there, we often went into the neighborhood and walked the streets in hopes of meeting our neighbors and creating the space to pray over the city. Those walks taught me to love inner city sidewalks—not the ones on the streets that were well-kept, crowded, and noisy with entertainment, but the ones just off the beaten path, tucked away in unknown neighborhoods. Those sidewalks told great stories.

As we walked, we paid close attention to where we stepped so we wouldn't trip on the many rifts and cracks. Most people hate those kinds of sidewalks, but hang on for a minute and let me explain why I came to love them.

The cracks in those sidewalks—where giant tree roots had pushed up the cement and exposed the ground—became one of my favorite parts of our walks. Those roots broke through only because there was a battle underground, a battle for new space as they twisted around and overlapped the roots of other trees. Sometimes in the overlap, there was a breakthrough. The pressure of the roots pushed and shifted and transformed the foundation, and the sidewalk was evidence of the battle.

What happens underground is so important. For a tree to truly go the distance in the city, it first has to go the distance under the city. Trees cannot exist only above ground. They have to go deep; it's how they survive.

That's how it is for us—what we see of our lives, what's on the surface, only makes up about 10 percent of who we are. The rest, the real, the 90 percent waits patiently under the surface. With just the right conditions and pressure, we will eventually break through. I didn't always know how important the underground work was until I turned my attention to what was below.

The root system that makes a tree a powerful presence in a community is like the root system that makes us a powerful presence in the Kingdom. Much of my life had been about what was happening above the surface—what I was producing, how I was performing, what people were seeing and ultimately saying. I didn't have time to look within. Nor did I really know how profitable it would prove to be.

*Above all else, guard your heart, for everything you do
flows from it,*
—Prov. 4:23

I knew I could survive on the side street, away from life. My survival wouldn't be about what I did above the surface; it would be how deep I went below the surface.

*But blessed is the one who trusts in the LORD,
   whose confidence is in him.
They will be like a tree planted by the water
   that sends out its roots by the stream.
It does not fear when heat comes;
   its leaves are always green.
It has no worries in a year of drought
   and never fails to bear fruit.*
—Jer. 17:7–8

Just before these two verses, Jeremiah wrote about the cursed bush, the one planted in the wastelands that never sees prosperity and is always parched. This cursed tree is known as the Ar'ar tree, and it is cursed because of what is not happening underground. It has a very shallow root system, which makes its location in the desert very troubling.

The roots of the Ar'ar tree go down deep enough to get some nutrients but not deep enough to get sustaining nutrients. The fruit of the tree is green and looks somewhat like a melon. But however good it looks, a hungry person opening the fruit of the Ar'ar tree is definitely disappointed because inside is nothing but a chalky, cobweb-like substance that no one, no matter how hungry they are, can fill up on. It is literally good for nothing. It gives the appearance of good, but inside it is rotten.

The blessed tree, however, produces beautiful, satisfying fruit because it has deep, sustaining roots. This tree doesn't have to fear when the heat comes or circumstances shift because what is developed underground sustains it enough to produce what it needs above ground.

Turning left was my invitation to go underground, to do some really important, deep root work—the kind that doesn't happen on the highways and byways of life. In the alley of my side street, I was digging up the lies of unbelief and replanting my heart in the soil of truth. My struggle to turn left was an underground issue. I trusted God enough to be where I currently was, but did I trust him enough to take me somewhere new? Could I let go of what I wanted and embrace where he invited me to go?

Everything we do springs forth from everything we are. Everything we are is determined by what our hearts actually believe. I wasn't turning left to go farther; I was turning left to go deeper.

Going deeper is not always easy for me. I'm a 3 on the Enneagram. That means I'm an achiever. At the core of my personality is someone who sets her mind to something and then does what it takes to obtain it. I am really good at trying harder. My first instinct when things are hard is to figure out how I can get better so the next time I can do better. But here's the problem with that. When it comes to this journey with Jesus, it's not about what we can do. My ability is still not enough. I will always fall short. That leaves me at a crossroads— do I spend my life trying to obtain something I can never reach, or do I learn to trust in someone who has reached me?

If God is always present and always at work, and if the always-present and always-working God cares more about my faith and my future than I do, then I don't have to try harder to do better because my journey is not about what I can or can't do above the surface. It's not on me to figure out where we are going and how I can help us get there. It's on me to go deeper—to put down healthy roots and develop a strong heart—to trust—to believe. A daughter fully convinced of her Father's love lives surrendered in obedience and expectation.

Thermostats vs. Thermometers

My change of pace enabled me to see what was under the surface. The Father and I had done a good work up until now, but my roots needed to go deeper for what was coming. No amount of trying harder would sustain me as the circumstances around me continued to change.

Here's the tension. There will be things above the surface that we need to do, but all the while God's focus is on what's happening beneath the surface. We cannot do the work of God without the grace of God. Everything we do is a by-product of who we are. Everything above is connected to everything below.

My bad days off the beaten path left me struggling to feel this new location. It was hard, and my feet were shaky. On the good days, I seemed to do okay. Back and forth I wobbled, kind of like a toddler learning to take his or her first steps.

God's promise to us is consistency—not that our circumstances will be consistent because our circumstances are always changing. But he promises us that in the midst of changing circumstances, our temperature will be consistent. We don't have to wobble just because the world wobbles.

There is a big difference between a thermostat and a thermometer. One dictates and controls temperature, and the other is controlled and dictated by temperature. We were created to be thermostats. Our hearts, rooted in the love of a really good Father, get to be steady and consistent, no matter the direction of our lives. We are invited to trust fully in what's developed within us.

As a Bible teacher, I knew that if I trusted God, I would follow him. So when push came to shove, I turned left. If I trusted God, I would embrace his invitation to this old firehouse on this unknown side street in Hamilton. If I trusted him, I would stop worrying about what I was or wasn't doing and lean into what he had already done. And so I did. I trusted in what was under the surface. My doing was evidence of my being. What was underground enabled me to go

forward, even when I didn't feel it. And each time I stepped forward
in faith, God took my trust deeper. I was growing because of who I
was becoming. I was becoming because of what I was doing.

Hand in hand, both of these things worked. The Hose House created the perfect external environment for my internal transformation.

The next time your circumstances change, why not pay attention
to your temperature? Are you steady when the wind picks up? Are
you constant when the water gets choppy? Are you consistent in loss
or in gain?

Behavior Management vs. Heart Transformation

> *But the LORD said to Samuel, "Do not look at his appearance*
> *or at his physical stature, because I have refused him. For the*
> *LORD does not see as man sees; for man looks at the outward*
> *appearance, but the LORD looks at the heart."*
>
> —1 Sam. 16:7 NKJV

This journey of discipleship doesn't happen on the highway
because it's not about what everyone else sees. When God looks at
you, he looks at your heart. If the outside of your life (what you do
and what you say) is inconsistent, it's because there is clutter on the
inside, and no amount of external work will set you free to walk with
the integrity you so desire.

> *Woe to you, teachers of the law and Pharisees, you*
> *hypocrites! You clean the outside of the cup and dish, but*
> *inside they are full of greed and self-indulgence. Blind*
> *Pharisee! First clean the inside of the cup and dish, and*
> *then the outside also will be clean.*
>
> —Matt. 23:25–26

Transformation from the outside in is nothing more than
behavior management. It's a quick fix to straighten our collars, shape

up our actions, and keep it together. It can be foreign to embrace what's under the surface, to dig deeper and expose true belief. Shame silences us, but grace beckons us to stop managing our behavior and start living in the reality of our untransformed hearts.

The best example I can give you is an honest look inside my home right now. My girls are great. They are kind, loving, thoughtful, and obedient. The level of parenting and restrictions I needed at their age far surpasses where they are. I love them, and I like them—a lot. However, there are moments when Ella can be really snippy with her younger sister, Addilyn.

I didn't have a sister, so I don't know what it's like to have someone sneak into your room and steal your favorite hoodie or walk out the door in your white crocs. I never got to fight over who got the upstairs movie room for the weekend sleepover or who was taking too much time in the bathroom. But I also never had a constant companion, someone I could cheer on and share life with. I may have an unrealistic expectation, but the story of sisterhood is meant to be a story of friendship. One day this will be my girl's story. They will be lifelong friends, but right now it's just all a struggle.

The mess above ground is due to a mess underground. My temptation as a parent is to manage Ella's behavior, to punish her when she is rude, essentially with the hope of forcing her to act differently. And there are consequences that do occur, but lately I've recognized my invitation is to go deeper, to look further into her heart. I can manage her behavior, or I can trust the Father to transform her heart.

Most days, I do my best to focus on heart transformation. I don't want to temporarily fix my girls' actions; I want God to permanently mend their hearts. A heart rooted in Christ manages itself. Behavior change is only temporary and will sell them short of who they were created to be, leaving them frustrated at their failures. Heart transformation allows them to live *from* a place of change and not *for* a place of change.

I try to dig deeper with my 15-year-old, and even though she hates my questions, she will admit that they help her see what's underneath.

"Ella, why do you think your first response to Addy is to be annoyed? Was her asking you to hand her a straw really such a daunting task for you? Would you answer your friend like that? What do you believe in your heart that drives you to respond to your sister like that?"

I want her to know the reason she does what she does. Every action is driven from something inside of her. We don't accidentally respond to our sister or our spouse with angst; we do it because somewhere inside of us lives angst, and it's seeping out. The inside is getting the outside dirty. So rather than excessively cleaning the outside, why don't we work on deeply cleaning the inside?

And you know what's happened in our home? As I've asked Ella questions, she has become more conscious of her posture, not always enough to change the behavior but enough to create space to go deeper. To be aware and to be present in reality is to set ourselves up for transformation. We can't change something we don't see.

One little lie on the inside can send us reeling on the outside. Behavior management allows us to live unaware of why we are actually doing what we are doing.

Your soul (or your heart) is the center of who you are. It's the inside you, the real you, the you others can't see. It's the part of you that brings life. It's also the part of you that can rob you of life if left unchecked.

Judah Smith in his book *How's Your Soul? Why Everything That Matters Starts with the Inside You* said it this way:

> Maybe our souls surprise us—but they don't surprise God. He isn't shocked or scandalized by the up-and-down tendencies of our hearts. He isn't embarrassed just because

our feelings get out of hand. He sees the craziness and chaos, and it doesn't bother him a bit. He knows us better than anyone, and he loves us more than everyone.[1]

I don't think we pay enough attention to our hearts. We shut them down, hoping our feelings don't get the best of us, and we press forward, doing what we have to do. Until we understand that we've been created in the image of God and given the keys to our emotional freedom, we will continue to live suppressed lives and miss out on the fullness of feeling and acting like Jesus.

External freedom and confidence, external victory and security come from internal connection and consistency. We know this truth in our physical lives. No one tries to live on fast-food cheeseburgers while expecting to be fit, happy, and healthy. We dedicate our time to eating right and exercising. We do what's good for us on the inside, knowing it will be displayed on the outside.

Peter Scazzero in his book *Emotionally Healthy Spirituality* put it this way:

> When I began to allow myself to feel a wider range of emotions, including sadness, depression, fear, and anger, a revolution in my spirituality was unleashed. I soon realized that a failure to appreciate the biblical place of feelings within our larger Christian lives has done extensive damage, keeping free people in Christ in slavery.[2]

Paying attention to what's happening on the inside is vital to changing what's happening on the outside. No matter how hard Ella might try to manage her behavior, she will eventually fail. We all will. Until she understands where her behavior comes from and surrenders it to the Father, she will stay stuck and eventually tire of trying to do better, thus slipping back into old postures and patterns.

God Doesn't Need Me to Shape Up

If God needed me to be good, then Jesus didn't have to die. God is the perfect parent, and his parenting doesn't change based on my imperfections. The belief that God needs anything from me in and of itself is false. He is God. He doesn't need me, and yet he wants me. It's bad news to live trying to obtain something we can't earn in hopes of gaining something we already have. We don't have to earn what he died to give us.

Look at the story of the rich young ruler.

> As Jesus started on his way, a man ran up to him and fell on his knees before him. "Good teacher," he asked, "what must I do to inherit eternal life?"
>
> "Why do you call me good?" Jesus answered. "No one is good—except God alone. You know the commandments: 'You shall not murder, you shall not commit adultery, you shall not steal, you shall not give false testimony, you shall not defraud, honor your father and mother.'"
>
> "Teacher," he declared, "all these I have kept since I was a boy."
>
> Jesus looked at him and loved him. "One thing you lack," he said. "Go, sell everything you have and give to the poor, and you will have treasure in heaven. Then come, follow me."
>
> At this the man's face fell. He went away sad, because he had great wealth.
>
> —Mark 10:17–22

Let me help you see what I am talking about. The rich young ruler has lived his life keeping all the rules. He's done it right. The outside of his cup shines brightly. His behavior is appropriate, and yet when he comes to Jesus and calls him "good teacher," Jesus stops him in his tracks.

Jesus has a point to make. The goodness he referenced was God. Only the Father has what it takes to be good. Jesus was good because he was perfectly centered in relationship with the Father. Any goodness in him was because of that connection. We are good because of God. God is everything good within us. Every good thing is God.

"For I know that good itself does not dwell in me, that is, in my sinful nature. For I have the desire to do what is good, but I cannot carry it out" (Rom. 7:18). We are born into sin, and the Old Testament proves that no amount of outer work will clean the inner issue. Jesus will always be what makes us good.

The other day, Addy asked me how I knew if God was speaking to me. She had an idea about something and wasn't sure if it was her idea or God's. "Is it a good idea, Addy?"

"I think so, Mom."

"Will it make someone feel loved and valued and cared for?"

"Yes," she answered without hesitation.

"Then it's God," I said, "because every good thing we have is from him. He is the author of the good in our lives."

Maybe the look on the rich young ruler's face told Jesus he didn't get it, because Jesus kept going. "You know the commandments," to which the rich young ruler stood up, proudly proclaiming the good he knew—"all these I have kept" (Mark 10:19–20).

But Jesus just loved him and told him to "go sell everything you have and give to the poor. . . . Then come, follow me" (Mark 10:21).

Imagine the look on the rich young ruler's face. It might have matched the surprise on my Addy's face when I told her that every good thing about her wasn't from her doing but from God's being. It's a humbling thing to know that all the good inside of you is because of Jesus and not anything you've done.

The rich young ruler had done the righteous thing all his life. He was overly careful, always keeping the commandments. And in the end, the amount of good he did externally didn't change who he was internally. We see that internally he relied on his wealth for his security. Internally, he served an idol, and his off-centered worship left him missing the mark entirely.

Every good thing you do is from God. Therefore, when something not good comes out of you, it means that something not from God has been poured into you. That's why this discipleship journey is never-ending. We are always going to need God's goodness. Part of turning left is about slowing down long enough to recognize what your actions really say. What you do is a reflection of who you are. As the disciples spent more time with Jesus, they started to become like Jesus. Clean the inside, and the outside will follow.

How's Your Heart?

Jesus knew the rich young ruler had the means to accomplish anything necessary to get himself into the Kingdom, but the one thing he needed to do (release the hold his finances had on him) he actually couldn't do. Why? Because his heart was in love with the security of his wealth and not the provision and protection of his Father.

When I struggle with obedience, I've learned to lay down my desire to fix or force it and instead try to figure it out. I befriend the struggle. What's going on in my heart that would cause it to be resistant to the invitation of my Father? Who am I trusting? Instead of trying harder, I come closer. In God's presence, I experience his goodness. His kindness in the midst of my reality almost always leads to my obedience. I want to follow him because he is kind. I want to obey him because he is good.

Your goodness is God in you. It will never depend on knowing more or doing better. It will always come from the amount of space he possesses in your heart.

The shadow of behavior management involves a lot of hiding. Lack of heart awareness creates a yo-yo out of life. Our reactions are inconsistent, to say the least. When we do good, we feel good, and when we do bad, we feel bad. Disappointment in our unpredictable behavior paves the road for this self-destructive pattern, eventually leading us to check out from God and his goodness altogether.

Does any of this ring a bell? Are there behaviors in your life you are working to manage? Are there things you are trying to do better, people you are trying to be gentle with? Are there places you wish you could go with God? Are there turns you keep trying to make? I hear your heart; there are things I want to do better, too, areas of my life in which I would love to look more like Jesus. The road there isn't paved by force. It's paved by following.

Instead of belittling your behavior, try befriending it. God doesn't want your behavior nearly as much as he wants your heart. A heart surrendered to God takes care of itself.

What if you laid down your felt-tip pen, stopped working so fervently toward a clean slate, and rested in the arms of the one who owns a slate that never gets dirty. God really doesn't need you to figure this one out. He's already paved your way to transformation. It's just a little to your left.

CHAPTER TWELVE

God Is Not in a Hurry

*Our longing for a way of life that works is most often
met with an invitation to more activity, which unfortunately
plays right into our compulsions and the drivenness of
Western culture.*

—Ruth Haley Barton

It takes time for our roots to go deeper. Some of the most important work you will do will be under the surface as you pay attention to both your circumstances and your temperature. The good news is that God is not in a hurry when it comes to our discipleship journey. He values every page, every chapter, and every section. Each is vitally important, and each plays a part in who we are becoming.

Ella is 15. That means that every day is a countdown to getting her license. She is constantly talking about being the last one in her grade to turn 16 and how she is going to spend the year bumming rides off of her friends so she isn't the only one still riding with Mom and Dad. She's in a hurry to get somewhere because she believes her arrival at that final destination will bring her greater contentment than where she is currently.

We all remember what that was like, knowing that a place of more freedom exists but it's not yet within our grasp. What she doesn't know is that getting her license will be great, but with it will come more work and responsibility. She will always have something more to look forward to. There will always be something ahead— graduation, college, graduate school, career, marriage, family— whatever future she pursues. There will always be more ahead than what she's left behind.

So you have Ella, who wants to drive, and then you have me, who wants this in-between time to last just a little bit longer. And why is that? Because I love having Ella and her friends in my car, even when it's inconvenient and sometimes keeps me up late at night.

Time is fast and fleeting. Life moves at such a rapid pace. The things we used to live in anticipation of are now slipping through our fingers, soon to be things of the past. It seems like just a few years ago that I was changing her diapers, and now I'm driving her to the homecoming dance or reminding her to be safe with her friends when I'm not around. I wish I could slow things down. I love where we are.

I've learned to savor the moment. More will come; it always does. But what if we don't get back today? In spite of all I've tried, life still goes on. Kids grow up. I get older.

I wonder if this is what it's like in the heart of the Father as we grow. I mean, he's a dad, right? And we are his children. Does he slow down because he understands how rushed time is and how quickly our formative years slip through his fingertips? Does he linger, wishing for just a little longer in each season, knowing that we'll never get to go back to what it was before? God knows the value of the unrushed life. In fact, he values it so much that he often invites us to turn left so we can slow down.

Pace Cars and High-Speed Lanes

The point of the highway is to save time. How do we get somewhere fast? We jump onto the highway, increase our speed, turn on cruise control, and wait for our exit. Busy cities have taken your typical three-lane highways to the next level, doubling the lanes, creating a car-pool lane, and setting suggested minimum speed requirements. All this is because life is happening, and many believe the best thing we can do is increase our speed in order to keep up.

There is work to be done, ladders to climb, and bills to pay. All those things make slowing down a threat to keeping up. We know from the GPS what it's like to be making good time, only to hear from the backseat, "I have to pee." You do a pit stop as quickly as you can, but by the time you merge back onto the highway, you have somehow lost six whole minutes of your estimated arrival time. This is a game for my husband—the challenge of making up for lost time.

You know what I spent the majority of my 20s aware of? What wasn't happening in my life. I wasn't all doom and gloom. I celebrated well and loved every good thing that came into my life—Jesus, marriage, babies, ministry—so many good, rich things that I am eternally grateful for. But somewhere in the back of my mind, there was this drive for the next thing moving me forward at an uncomfortably fast pace. I think I believed a place existed where, once I got there, I could slow down, let up, and enjoy myself a bit more.

Once I graduated from college.
Once I got married.
Once I found a job.
Once I figured out what I was good at.
Once I got really good at what I was good at.
Once I had a family.
Once my babies slept through the night.
Once my kids were in school all day.
Once my kids didn't need so much of my help.

It created a life of speeding past present moments in pursuit of perfect moments.

There was a lie inside of me that a future version of myself was more valuable than the current version of myself.

Rushed Wanderings

Jesus's disciples felt this tension, too—the pull of wanting to get where they were going more quickly. In fact, in their struggle, they often tried to get Jesus to more rapidly advance himself onto the throne, to reveal himself and his divinity before it was time. It was so tempting that even Jesus's mother fell victim to it.

All of them were at a wedding at Cana in Galilee when the wine ran out. Scripture says that Jesus's mother approached him, concerned over what that would mean for the host's family. It was disgraceful to run out of wine while guests were still present. Jesus's mother knew what would help. She called her son near and said, "They have no more wine." "Woman, why do you involve me?" Jesus replied. "My hour has not yet come" (John 2:3–4). Still, Jesus's mother pressed in until Jesus instructed the servants to fill the wine jars with water and give them to the master of the banquet. When the servants drew the water out, it became wine.

Jesus turned water into wine even though it wasn't his time yet. The many miracles that were ahead for him and his family would pave his road to the cross, but in a moment of panic, his mother outs him and fast-tracks his plans. Being content with where we are while embracing the tension of where we head is a real thing, and it's okay to dance in that tension. We can look forward to what's ahead while appreciating what is now, both at the same time.

When the only objective in your life is to get to your next destination, you miss out on the impact of your current situation. On the other side of my left turn, I began to realize how quickly I had been running. It took months to slow down my breathing and steady my heart. I was running so fast that I actually lost sight of the amazing things happening around me every day. I didn't want to get to the end of this, look back, and realize I was running from the very place I was intended to be.

Overbooked and Overlooked

The pace of life for me at the mega church was fast. I moved quickly from one thing to the next, constantly cramming too many meetings into a day. I found my significance in an overbooked and overly busy schedule. I worshiped the god of time. He did not bend to me; I bent to him. He controlled me, overworked me, and still somehow always seemed to disappoint me. He kept me on my phone attending to someone else's issue while holding up a finger, ignoring my own. I put aside the things I loved to do for the things time loved me to do. If fun was profitable, fine, but if fun was just fun, then I didn't have time.

I was going somewhere and actually on pace to get there quickly. I believed arriving at this unknown destination would give me more of something I didn't have but obviously needed. Maybe you get what I am talking about. Maybe you are living for the day you are finally married or have kids out of diapers. Maybe you hope for your toddlers to be more independent or for your teenagers to grow up and be more responsible. I have friends having babies and friends who just sent both of their grown boys into the real world and are experiencing the reality of an empty nest. One thing remains the same across the board. Time doesn't slow down. We do.

And so we can wait for something outside of us to change so something inside of us can change. Or we can turn left, follow Jesus off the beaten path, and become a person who rests well, knowing that sometimes in our rest, the most important work is taking place.

Time moved very slowly at the Hose House. It was foreign to me. People were always outside, sitting on their porches. People were present. At first I struggled in the sitting. When I struggled, I worked. I cleaned, prepped the walls for paint, or reorganized the broken furniture. I did whatever I could to not just sit. Eventually, the pace of slow got the best of me, and I learned to just be present.

Dave learned, too, and he is the busiest person I know. His capacity to fill life is more than anything I've ever seen. He honestly gets more done in a day than I sometimes do in a week. But he was different at the Hose House. After he lost his job at the mega church, he told me he was committing to not working for the rest of the summer—three months. He said he knew that was part of his invitation from the Father, to rest his way into the next season. I'm still shocked that he did it. In fact, he actually did it so well that sometimes I couldn't get him to do what I needed him to do.

It makes me think of how a pendulum swings. When it's dropped, it swings high to each side, going back and forth and back and forth until the momentum dies down and it ends up perfectly centered. This is how it works with hurry. When we live in the fast lane and drive at the speed of light, always rushing from one thing to the next, our left turn into the alley can feel like an abrupt change of pace. Swinging high to the other side isn't the problem. I think the Father sometimes swings us high to the other side so we can experience rest in its entirety, only to eventually rhythmically lead us into a more middle place of posture.

The Highway to Hana

We recently experienced this same thing with our family on vacation. After Dave and I got married, we went to Maui on our honeymoon. I don't remember putting a lot of thought into it at the time, just that there was an amazing, all-inclusive package deal available a few weeks after we got engaged. It seemed good, so we booked it, and I promptly turned my attention to our big day. Maybe Dave thought about the honeymoon more than I did. All I can remember was spending hours on wedding planning, sampling cakes, and trying on dresses.

We stepped off the plane in Hawaii unprepared. Sometimes, unplanned vacations are exactly what we need. When life is chaotic and crazy, unplanned vacations invite us to retreat and rest. We make a habit of doing this as a family because Dave's parents have a condo in Florida that makes it easy to just show up. But in the case of our honeymoon, we were unplanned and unprepared.

Tired from a long flight and lack of sleep, we were only half thinking.

Dave put his wallet and keys down on a table as our hotel clerk walked us into our room to show us the view and ask if we had any questions. It was the next morning as we got ready to go to breakfast (at 5:00 a.m. because that was 10:00 a.m. at home, and I was starving) that we realized Dave's wallet was missing. It wasn't on the table where he had put it or anywhere else in the room.

Hours later, after lots of searching and conversations with the front desk employees, his wallet showed up in the parking lot—with no money but still full of his credit cards and license.

After that first-day fiasco, we determined not to allow it to ruin our trip and woke up early the next day to drive the Road to Hana. It appeared to be a tourist must-do. The Road to Hana was exactly what it said—a road to Hana, a small community in Maui. Other than a black beach, there wasn't actually much to do in Hana. But it wasn't Hana itself that drew people. It was the journey there.

The Road to Hana twists its way up beautiful, rocky cliffs while the waves of the Pacific Ocean crash into the rocky sides and then throw themselves back wildly. Every few miles there were breathtaking stops for photo ops and opportunities to swim in waterfalls. At the top of our climb was a bamboo forest with bamboo as tall as the buildings back home. Everything about it was beautiful.

If you asked Dave, he would tell you the best part of our journey was the backside of the Road to Hana. You could only drive on those roads if you had a four-wheel-drive vehicle, and littered along the way were warning signs about one-lane dirt roads and steep cliffs. We made our way up impossible cliffs and across wooden bridges that brought so much tension to my back that it felt like it was breaking in two, and yet it was the most beautiful scenery I had ever seen in my entire life. We spent the entire day driving up and down those winding roads. It's my favorite memory of our time there together.

Two summers ago, we surprised our girls with a family vacation to Maui. For years we had talked about how much we wanted to go back and relive our honeymoon, and Ella's 13th birthday seemed like the perfect time to do it. This time, with a little more life experience under my belt, I researched what a family of four should do in Maui. I read about the best places to eat, beaches to visit, and excursions to book.

When I pulled up the Road to Hana, what I learned blew my mind. There was information for every single stop. Everything we could see and even the things we couldn't see were written about and available to us. I spent days researching that little, winding road we had traveled so unaware of just 13 years before. I marked the places we needed to stop and get out. I circled potential lunch stops, beach breaks, and tourist must-dos. This time, it wasn't about getting through the Road to Hana as much as it was about getting the Road to Hana through us.

I didn't want my girls to only know it the way I knew it. Even though driving the road 13 years before had been amazing, Dave and I, in our rush and inexperience, had missed so much. We just didn't know what we didn't know, so we had focused on getting to the end. We had pushed forward to the finish line thinking the best part was ahead when actually the best part was always there, right in front of us.

With the girls, we were so different. We stopped every chance we got. We explored wilderness paths, swam in the waterfalls, and took pictures. We lingered. We visited the beach, played in the black sand, stopped to see a toucan by the side of the road, and got out for pineapple freezes. We did so much, in fact, that by the time we got to Hana, we didn't have time to stay because it would be too dark to drive the backside of the road safely. We almost needed another day.

On our honeymoon, I was aware of the beauty, but I didn't stop long enough to let it take my breath away. Lingering on the road made all the difference in the world. The unrushed pace of not caring when we got to our next mile marker gave my girls the freedom to explore. The journey felt restful and satisfying. I didn't know the beauty that it actually held until I paused long enough to hold it.

God's Not in a Hurry

Here's the good news for you about discipleship. God is not in a hurry. Jesus didn't rush the disciples, and he is not rushing you. He is not a slave to time. He actually created and controls it. And because he knows the end game, he's surrendered to the present purpose. You don't have to fear falling behind because of your left turn.

There's so much available to you right where you are—so many waterfalls to swim in and scenery to experience. You will surely miss out on life if you only live to get somewhere rather than live because you are somewhere. This has been the most tangible change in my life throughout this journey. Leaving my job at a mega church was like taking the exit ramp off the highway. The change in speed was instant and obvious. But making my way onto the less crowded and unpopular side streets didn't cost me nearly as much as I thought it would. In the end, it was a small price to pay to recover my life.

Dave's last weekend at the church was almost six months to the day after mine. Remember our emotional goodbyes, our tears and laughter? Remember how we walked out the door and into the parking lot, climbed into Dave's truck, and headed for a week at the lake? That was the only way we knew how to resist the temptation to anxiously enter into figuring out what would be next and to rest. On the water that week, life slowed down, and we settled in. The girls tubed and knee boarded behind the boat as Dave pulled them around for hours, and I deeply enjoyed having all my people in one place.

Most people don't go on vacation when they've gone from being a two-income family to a zero-income family in a matter of six months, but everything about resting well felt right to us. This was our left turn, our chance to slow down, step off the beaten path, and wait for what was next.

The Bible says, "Since we are living by the Spirit, let us follow the Spirit's leading in every part of our lives" (Gal. 5:25 NLT). We were following his lead. On our own, we would have spent our time looking for jobs while trying to figure out what to do next, but synced with God, we remembered that he already knew and had promised to show us when the timing was right.

Outside of family and covenant relationships, there will be seasons when you run with people and seasons when you run without people. Neither is wrong, and both are good. This was a season we would run with very few people on a road not many would travel. My yes in this season meant saying no to so many of the people we had run previous miles with. These were necessary pauses. Our journeys are individualized learning plans prepared strategically with us in mind. The Father knew what we needed, and if he led us away, I could trust it was for our benefit.

When I turned left, the hill I needed to climb was massive and littered with debris, both physically and spiritually. It forced me to slow down. I could not make my way through this dark alley at the same pace I ran on the highways just a few months prior. It would destroy me. As I slowed down, the rest of the world seemed to keep going. I will be honest with you, it hurt to see my friends and family run on without me, but I let go of them and held on to Jesus, and we learned to step forward together.

The lie that I wasn't making good enough time doesn't hold me back anymore. In fact, most days I don't worry about the time I keep because I'm attached to the keeper of time. He will get me where he needs me to be right when I need to be there. I am ready and available. I'm paying attention and living in obedience. But I'm also fully present and basking in the mundane moments of life; it's beautiful and breathtaking, and I don't want it to move so quickly.

Close Your Eyes

You aren't missing anything. You don't have to go so fast. You are not behind. There's still time. You're not too old. You can slow down and enjoy the drive. You can even close your eyes for a bit if you want. No one is keeping time. You aren't going to be overlooked. You don't have to be everywhere. You don't have to do everything.

If Hose House #4 taught me anything, it taught me that letting go and holding on go hand in hand. It's about a responsible dependency. I let go and held onto God, trusting that what he hands me is what I need. The picture is one of holding on with open hands, tightly so we don't lose pace but not so tightly so God is free to move what we're holding onto.

God instructs us, "Be still, and know that I am God" (Ps. 46:10). I'm sure you've heard this verse time and time again in reference to rest. And it's true. Being still is important in our lives and on this journey. But that's not exactly what God is implying in this particular verse.

God is not interested only in our outer stillness because we can be still and be stuck. He is focused on our inner stillness. He longs for our hearts to trust in his hand, and sometimes, he will still our lives with the intention of ultimately stilling our hearts. Other versions of this passage use the words *cease striving*. The Hebrew word is *raphah*, which implies a good deal more than just sitting quietly. To better understand God's perspective, we need to see the other uses of this form of the verb.

Joshua 10:6 translates *raphah* as *abandon*.
Deuteronomy 4:31 uses *destroy*.
Psalm 37:8 uses *refrain*.

What is the similarity? In every case, this form of *raphah* carries the idea of letting go of something. That's the imagery we need in Psalm 46:10. God is not asking us to be quiet and sit down. He is asking us to let go and trust. He commands us to stop the striving, frantic business of living and requests our full and undivided attention. Then, and only then, will the second part of the verse become reality. If we want to know and be confident that He is God, it comes on the other side of our *raphah*.

God is the God of your life, and his lordship is best recognized on the other side of our *raphah*, our surrender, our letting go. Perhaps there's an invitation for you to let go of time today.

Part Three

THE INVITATION TO TEACH

CHAPTER THIRTEEN

Old Path, New Person

Our vision is rarely radically changed all at once;
it is usually altered and informed over time by these tools.
Journeying well doesn't necessarily mean knowing the
directions or understanding what it means to walk;
it means being informed by the one who
does know these things.

—Kyle Strobel

Eventually, my left turn brought me back to the original path
and presented me with the opportunity to turn left again
and pick up almost right where I stepped off. My run off
the beaten path and up the hill took me away, but it also brought
me back. Where I was and how I used to serve felt so close and
familiar, but at the same time, who I had become and how I would
now journey forward were miles and miles apart. Transformation
took root in my heart, and there was no going back.

I could step back onto the old path, but I would be doing it as a new person. When knowledge turns to experience, it leaves your head and changes your heart. That kind of change is forever with you. I cannot unknow what I have come to know about my Father and the lavish way he loves and purses me.

Until I took my left turn, I knew God as the one in charge. I worked for him, and he took care of me. It was a good transaction. Following Jesus off the beaten path opened me up to a new connection, one that would have an impact on me forever.

Jesus knew the Father differently. Perhaps that is why others were so drawn to Jesus. For so many decades, people had just been told what rules to follow, where to go or not go, when to sacrifice, and how to sacrifice. They always had to do something to access God.

Jesus showed people a different way. He pulled them into the heart of the Father by loving and accepting them right where they were and yet inviting them into even more. Through Jesus, God became the provider, the rescuer, the redeemer, the best story-writer, the friend, the brother. Through Jesus, God became grace and truth. Through Jesus, God made himself known, and the journey took a significant shift.

Jesus has invited us into this crazy journey. He's put his hand out to us like a good big brother and welcomed us to turn left, step off the beaten path, and get to know the love of the Father in a way that only he can show us. Discipleship is the slow cooking of our faith. It doesn't unfold overnight but rather day in and day out as we embrace the journey to what we don't know. Great theologian Eugene Peterson described the journey of discipleship as a long obedience in the same direction.

Where's Waldo?

When we were little, my brother and I spent hours searching through the *Where's Waldo?* books. Our eyes scanned crowded pages hoping to catch a glimpse of Waldo in his red and white shirt, jeans, and matching hat. Most of the time, Waldo carried a cane that sometimes stood out best. Page after page, we raced to spot him first, pointing and proclaiming the minute one of us recognized him. Then we would turn the page and start the game all over again. Sometimes, Waldo was in the middle of a crowded desert, and other times, he was on the Mediterranean Sea or shopping in a crowded mall. Page after page after page, we searched to find our friend. It was a trip until you reached the end of the book.

But there was one problem with the *Where's Waldo?* books. Once you found Waldo, you could always find Waldo. No matter how hard you tried to erase your memory you couldn't unsee what you had seen. Still to this day I could probably pick up one of those books, and my mind would take me back to the general area where Waldo hid. Or maybe I wouldn't. Maybe I wouldn't remember where Waldo was now that I have spent so many years away from him. I'm not sure I could instantly recognize his striped shirt and little walking stick. But back in the day when it was fresh, no matter how hard I tried to pretend, I just couldn't forget it.

This reminds me of the way the Father works. He is pages and pages deep of goodness. There are so many aspects and characteristics worth discovering about him. Throughout the different pages of our lives, he waits patiently for us to recognize him in a different light, through a new lens. He is different on every page, but at the same time, he is exactly what we need on every page.

We don't forget what we knew about him before. As long as we stay present in our connection, discipleship is only about gaining more insight into his characteristics. He is layer upon layer.

My left turn took me to a new page. That new page looked unknown and confusing. I didn't recognize anything on it, and worse yet, I seemed to have left every familiar thing I loved on the previous page. But the longer I stayed on a new page, the more my eyes adjusted and the more he drew me in. Not only did I find him there, but I found everything that came with him.

The best part is that I didn't lose what I discovered on the previous pages. I didn't forget who he was before this page. I only added to it. I know people who don't turn the page for fear of losing what they have on their current page, as though God were asking them to give up something he didn't intend to give back. That's just not the way it works. If God is asking for something, it's only because he has something more to give on the other side. Your release, your surrender, opens you up for him to deliver it.

Things on this new page were different, which meant things on the old page were different. But different is not the enemy. If we are on a journey of becoming more and more like Jesus, then we are going to change. The person you are today will not be the person you know 10 years from now. Discipleship has done its job if you are different. Sometimes, your inner changes will drive your outer changes, and sometimes, it will be the other way around. God is not privy to one or the other; he's dedicated to you and this process of transformation.

The gospel is always about multiplication. Even when fruit is pruned from the Vine in John 15, it is pruned so more fruit can grow in its place. The temporary loss is just that—temporary. Soon, the empty branch will be stronger and full of even more abundant fruit.

The loss of turning the page was temporary in my life. I mourned friendships and ministry events, opportunities and traditions, but I also discovered new ones along the way. My left turn exposed me to a side of God that I didn't know existed. I didn't know what a good Father he was. I didn't realize how much he liked me and longed to be with me or that this life wasn't only the sum of how much I would sacrifice for him. Before I turned left, I hadn't experienced the fullness of my present moment and the peace in trusting that he holds tomorrow. I knew God was my redeemer and rebuilder, but now I know him as my Father and my friend.

It's something I could only learn from Jesus because it's the thing he knows all about. He turned left and came here to be like us. On his new page, he leaned in and trusted his Father to be faithful in the midst of alarming circumstances. When things began to shake, he held steady, knowing relationship would bring him through. And he did it. He turned left and conquered death.

Jesus knows the Father in every way, and each time He invites us to turn left, he is inviting us into a new dimension of encounter and experience. *Where's Waldo?* took your search to another level once you reached the back of the book and realized an invitation to go back to each page and search for the things Waldo had dropped along the way—sunglasses, backpack, shoe, towels, snacks, you name it. You might find these things on a Waldo page. I think in the later books you could even search for his brother and sister.

This is significant to me because on our pages of life, we don't just find God and move on. With him come many other things. Each page is full of blessing, battles, and breakthroughs. Some are hard and intense and take every ounce of energy we've mustered. Others are light and airy, inviting us to run downhill for a bit while God replenishes our breath. Regardless of what we find, they each make up the landscape of our lives—pages we will never forget, stories we will never cease to tell. Miracles, blessings, insight, wisdom, battles, pain, hope, joy—page after page we turn, each new page adding a significant piece to our story.

From One House to Another

Hose House #4 was no different. It was a much needed page in my life, a left turn that introduced me to a new understanding of God as Father and a new depth in myself as a daughter, disciple, mother, pastor, speaker, and author. What I now know I could not unknow. I discovered another side of God, and I was in love. I was a new person, and just like that I found myself on the brink of another left turn.

The Hose House worked as our church. There we created space to worship and connect with the Father, with one another, and with the world around us. As a family, we were living on mission, and it felt right. Periodically, Dave and I would take our girls to a church down the street so they could experience some of what we knew as a "normal" church. Ella was able to be part of their kids worship team, and Addy loved seeing all her school friends on the weekends. Dave and I were good friends with some of the staff, and it felt like a safe place for us to be while we searched for all God was writing on this unknown page.

I will be really honest with you. I didn't know a lot of what God was doing and how long we would be on this side street in Hamilton doing an out-of-the box ministry. The gentleman who gifted us the Hose House gave it to us for five years. At the end of those five years, the deal was to give it back to him because he planned to restore the building as part of his retirement dream. A year and a half in, Dave and I were keenly aware that God had brought us there to give us some specific things.

First, God showed me that he is the giver of all good things. We turn every page because of what he longs to give and not because of what we have to offer. So often I thought he took me places because he wanted to use me, to use my gifts and my strengths. The tension of the Hose House was that everything I knew how to give wouldn't work, so I could do nothing but receive. I stopped showing up to work and simply showed up as God worked.

I also realized that his Father's heart is never to use his children. He didn't create me just so he could spend me. His Father's heart is to be with his children, to give to them, provide for them, and partner alongside them. Ministry isn't about what I have to give; it's about all God longs to offer. The greatest thing I had to give was a transformation from within.

At the Hose House, I learned to slow down and receive because everything would come together when it was supposed to come together and not a moment before. The gift of the Hose House was the realization that what the Father does in me he will also do through me, and if I open my life up to encountering him, I will in turn become an encounter for others to experience his goodness.

Bill Johnson, author of *Manifesto for a Normal Christian Life*, put it this way:

> That depth at which he goes in me determines how far he goes out of me. It's a personal encounter. It's not our commitment to healing. It's not our commitment to evangelism. It's not our commitment to any of these things. It's our commitment to the person, to live faithfully with a person.[1]

I still offered a lot while we were there. We worked, and we worked hard, but the beauty of being in such a broken place is a keen awareness of how incapable we are of providing the restoration necessary for life to abound. Our friends on the streets didn't need our temporary assistance. They needed an eternal encounter. Only the love of the Father could give them hope. It wasn't ours to determine how and when they turned; it was simply ours to offer.

I encountered God in new ways there, and from this place of overflow in my heart, others were being drawn in. It was not because of anything I was doing but simply because of all God was being.

One particular Sunday as we visited our friends' church with the girls, Dave leaned over close to me during worship and whispered, "I can't help but feel like we are supposed to plant a church." Planting a church was the farthest thing from my mind. It was honestly something we'd never discussed before. "Dave," I sighed, "someone would have to show up at my front door and tell me they wanted us to plant a church with them for me to think that's what God wants to do." The idea of going back to the old path at that point sounded exhausting. We had just found our footing, and we were just now getting good at this.

He shrugged his shoulders and went back to singing. Later that night, I got a text message from Alton, one of our long-time friends and ministry partners. We served with Alton during our time at the Cincinnati Vineyard. Our families had experienced so much depth together in just a few short years. Alton said he needed to meet with Dave and me and wanted to know how soon we could be available. The next morning at 7:00, Alton walked through our doorway, sat down at our table, and started talking. "We are going to plant a church, and we want you two on board with us. Be on our leadership team. Help us make disciples and grow a family."

I laughed at his invitation because of my conversation with Dave the day before. We looked at each other, and I shrugged my shoulders and said, "We're in!" I think Alton was shocked by the quickness of my response, but when I explained to him the previous day's conversation, he laughed and welcomed us onboard. We were going to plant a church. As we sat around the table with a fresh awareness of who God was and a new eagerness to share our findings with the world around us, it became more and more clear that the best way for us to lead others off the beaten path was to plant a church.

Over the next few months, the vision and direction of Anthem House Church was birthed within our small core team. We sat in kitchens and living rooms in prayer and worship asking God to give us wisdom and insight beyond our abilities and understanding.

The decision was to launch Anthem in our town. All of us lived in the same vicinity and interacted with the community on a daily basis. It made sense for us to take advantage of our deep roots to make disciples right where we lived. People knew us here, and they trusted us. We saw them at soccer games and at dance studios. They shopped with us and gathered with us at local football games.

The gift of the Hose House was the space and grace for my personal transformation. It was the time allotted to stop focusing so much on making disciples and rest in my own personal process of becoming a disciple. From this new place of connection and understanding, I now had something different to offer the same old path I'd left behind.

Turning the Page

It's extremely interesting to me how Jesus led me away from something, all the while intending to bring me back to the same thing. I've already pointed out how this is a practical parenting technique. When we were parents of toddlers, how many times did we redirect them from things that could seemingly bring harm, knowing that someday soon they would be able to handle these very things? God didn't take these things away from me; he took me away from them. My time away allowed me to grow. I was coming back stronger and more solidified in my identity than I even knew was possible.

Forever and Always

Maybe it's just me, but until now I have been very finite in my thinking. Everything in my mind was forever. If I did something, I assumed it would always be what I would do. If I believed something, I thought I would always believe it. If I learned something, the idea of unlearning was lost to me. My left turn taught me that life is not really either-or as much as it is both-and.

God will work in me, and he will work through me. He will teach me some things before I teach others, and other times I will learn on the other side of teaching others. We want life to be this straight, consecutive, sequential line when the reality is that our journey with Jesus is all over the place, and that's exactly as it's meant to be. As we follow him, he works in us. What he does in us will ultimately seep out of us, causing the world around us to be impacted. The longer we journey, the more we love and the less we know. Jesus is infinite and beyond our understanding. The end of him is always beyond reach, and yet our journey toward him grows deeper and richer with every turn.

> *As the heavens are higher than the earth, so are my ways*
> *higher than your ways and my thoughts than your thoughts.*
> —Isa. 55:9

Learning, unlearning, relearning—it's all part of the process, and it's all part of our growth. We don't have to understand. We don't have to figure it out. We don't have to know it all. In fact, rest assured that we are not capable of knowing it all.

Nicodemus was a synagogue ruler, but he was intrigued by the message Jesus taught. He was drawn in, but to go in would surely put him out among the other leaders sitting at his table. Still, he had to know more about this message that Jesus taught.

> *[Nicodemus] came to Jesus at night and said, "Rabbi, we know that you are a teacher who has come from God. For no one could perform the signs you are doing if God were not with him."*
>
> *Jesus replied, "Very truly I tell you, no one can see the kingdom of God unless they are born again."*
>
> *"How can someone be born when they are old?" Nicodemus asked. "Surely they cannot enter a second time into their mother's womb to be born!"*
>
> —John 3:2–4

Nicodemus knew this in his head but had not received it in his heart. He knew Jesus was from God; the signs and miracles were evidence of that. But it wasn't making sense in his heart. This is the tension of learning to trust. Without relationship, Nicodemus would never be able to navigate the gap between what he knew and what he felt.

Jesus is the way, but his ways don't always make sense. When we struggle to understand the what, our invitation is to trust in the who. In order to do that, Nicodemus needed to be born again. He needed to relearn how to be a child with a really good and kind Father. Growing up under God the Father would establish in him the foundation necessary for him to go forward differently.

This perfectly describes the rebirth our family went through while we were at the Hose House. We wrestled with shifting shadows until our old paradigms gave way and our new understanding took deeper root. From a place of new rootedness, we could now go back to the old path, capable of handling a more abundant fruit.

The work of relationship put in on that side street would provide the strength necessary for the next page of our journey. And just like that, two years after launching into street ministry at the Hose House, our family handed over our keys to Daniella and the rest of the leadership team and ventured back on the path to grow a church family. It was clear to us that our time there was finished. We received what God longed to give. This place served as his breeding ground for our transformation, and now we would return to the old path and new people.

The Discipleship Story

This was like the journey of Jesus's disciples. They left everything to follow him off the beaten path. Each time Jesus ministered in their presence, what they knew in their heads counteracted what they were experiencing in their hearts, and they were left with the option to believe the new. Over and over again, they abandoned old ways of thinking for new ways of living.

It was a far from perfect journey, and that should give us great hope. Back and forth they wrestled to deep-root themselves in identity and relationship. As sons of a really good Father, they could walk with the same power and authority as their teacher. Some days, they believed and operated well in this new mindset, and other days, their surrounding circumstances proved too difficult to navigate, leaving them doubtful and struggling.

I'm thankful for real-life examples—a group of men (12 disciples) who wanted it with all they had but still struggled to fully receive it. I'm encouraged at all God will do in and through us as we learn to walk forward as sons and daughters. This is, in fact, the system he put in place to change the world. It was his idea to do this through discipleship.

And that brings me back to *your* left turn. Is there a place in your life that you sense Jesus leading you—not because of what you do or don't have to give but because of what he longs for you to receive? Is there a turn you need to make? Is there a season of rebirth and renewal that needs some space on your calendar? What might God be inviting you into? What might he be calling you away from?

Or maybe you have already turned, but those shadowy alleys got the best of you and you found yourself right back at those places and spaces you previously left behind. It's not too late to turn again. God doesn't waste any of your time. He will make the best of all you give him. Thankfully, discipleship is not a story of people doing this journey perfectly; it is a story of people who did it presently. What is your invitation . . . presently? And what are you going to do about it . . . presently?

CHAPTER FOURTEEN

Practice Makes Permanent

*The best guide for any journey is one who has
made the journey himself or herself—perhaps multiple
times—and thus knows something about the terrain, the
climate, the beauties, dangers and challenges present at
each point along the way.*

—Ruth Hailey Barton

I have a good friend who is a soccer coach for a local club in our area. She knows her stuff when it comes to player development. Growing up, I learned how to play soccer in the backyard by just kicking the ball around. There was a spot on the side of my house that was perfect for shooting, as long as I hit the ball on the bricks. If I was off by just a little, the ball would slam into the siding of the house with a loud thud, and moments later my mom would appear outside to remind me that people have to live in this house.

All day, every day, I kicked the soccer ball. Day and night, I was out there for hours, dribbling up and down the backyard, kicking it as hard as I could against the brick, working on crosses and penalty kicks, juggling, and head balls. I practiced by myself and with my neighbors. Occasionally, I would drag the kids I babysat out into the backyard so they could be the goalies while I drilled the ball at their little outstretched arms.

All that practice made soccer permanent in my mind. Playing soccer became simply about repetition. I never had speed and agility, Coerver training, or technical and tactical sessions. I just kicked and dribbled, shot and juggled over and over and over until I could do it in my sleep.

I was a good soccer player because I played a lot of soccer. I played it all the time. I got out of bed thinking about soccer and went to bed thinking about soccer. My life centered on one main thing: soccer. My singlemindedness in regard to soccer formed me into a good soccer player.

It works like that in discipleship, too. You know why I am good at discipleship? Because, just like soccer was when I was growing up, discipleship is what I spend my life doing now. I practice it. I talk about it. I read about it. I pray about it. I think about it, and I reproduce it. People sometimes comment on how this discipleship journey sounds simple coming out of my mouth, and I say, "It didn't always come so naturally."

Over the years as I've pursued one thing above all else, repetition has paved an easy path in my mind. Disciple is who I am, and discipleship is what I do. These are the lenses I wear. I rarely take them off, and thus I tend to see fairly consistently. When I view life through the lens of discipleship, everything becomes an opportunity to grow, learn, and develop.

Permanent, Not Perfect

Remember my good friend Sarah? She says that practice makes permanent, not to be confused with perfect because if perfection is the goal, then we will always fall short. We don't have the ability to and we will never get this life perfect. It's not how the story goes. God's rescue mission was planned in such a way that constant, continued relationship would be necessary. We need God. We will always need him. This is not about teaching you something so you can get it right and he can move on. This is about unity and dependency, relationship and responsibility.

That being said, I love the way Sarah puts it: Practice makes permanent. She's talking about the pathways in our brains. The more you do something, the more easily you will do something. Every thought that enters our minds has to be accounted for, even the ones we aren't aware of. They all go somewhere. When we make a decision to trust God instead of a decision to trust ourselves, that decision is made in our minds. What we decide in our mind shapes the paths in our brains.

> *We demolish arguments and every pretension that sets itself up against the knowledge of God, and we take captive every thought to make it obedient to Christ.*
>
> —2 Cor. 10:5

What happens in your alleys is that you start to capture wrong thoughts and redirect them down right pathways. In her book *Switch on Your Brain*, Caroline Leaf writes, "As we think, we change the physical nature of our brain. As we consciously redirect our thinking, we can wire out toxic patterns of thinking and replace them with healthy thoughts."[1]

Your thoughts always travel the quickest route from A to B. That means when a thought drops into your mind, it will find the easiest road to travel (the highway), merge on, and make its way into an action. There's a whole lot more to this if you study neuroscience. It's technical and really smart, but for the sake of not losing you in all the details, I'm going to stick with practice makes permanent.

Addy has played soccer for eight years now, and this year it finally clicked. In order to get better with her left foot, she is going to have to practice with her left foot. You know what that means? It means she has a foot that is naturally better, a foot she can kick with harder and more directly—one she can control—and she isn't going to use it. She is going to deny what comes naturally and practice with what is unnatural. And the more she does it, the more she will be able to do it. Her left foot capabilities will grow as her practice allows them to.

There are some lies you believe that you don't even recognize until you step off the beaten path. I've shared many of mine with you throughout the pages of these chapters. I thought God loved me more when I did more. I thought he needed me to slave myself for him. I was convinced that I was only as valuable as my last good sermon or ministry-driven idea. All of these lies traveled well-worn highways in my brain, leading me to do and act in certain ways.

My left turn brought me into direct conflict with these lies. As I lingered in the shadows, I realized that if God really needed me to perform in order to earn his affection, I was in trouble. When I practiced doing nothing and discovered an even more radical love of my Father, I began to pave a new pathway. Each new pathway was full of freedom and good news.

This is how it works with our faith. There is a level of comfort you have with what you know, with where you've been, and with how you've grown. No doubt, God has done a mighty work in you throughout your journey together. But he will do more. In fact, he will always do more. There is no end to his goodness. We will never run out of opportunities to turn left and learn something new about God.

Let's Call It Practice

Addy asked me just the other day if the US women's soccer team held practices. It's a valid question. They are the best women's soccer team in the world and have proven so multiple times. Why, then, do they need to practice?

They practice because practice makes permanent. It doesn't make perfect because perfection is not attainable. But each player sets out to hone a skill to such a level that it comes naturally and automatically. The players are naturally good at soccer, not because they were born with the ability to strike a ball at just the right angle and place it in the upper right corner of the net, out of reach for even the best goalies. They didn't wake up one day and possess an elite level of ball movement skills. They practiced, and they practiced, and they practiced.

They practiced again and again until their muscle memory was so comfortable traveling the pathway of juggles and ball cuts that it happened automatically. Now they keep practicing because this is true: What you don't use, you will lose.

Our faith is practice. It's real life, and yet it's not. This is a practice run for what it will be like to worship continually in the presence of God. One day, every knee will bow in heaven and on earth. One day, walking in step with God will be all we do all the time, and we won't even have to study or think about it. One day, there will be no more tension between good and evil because it will all just be good. But for now, we practice. We use the authority and the keys Jesus has given us and bring heaven to earth—not perfectly, but presently. Lysa TerKeurst says it well:

> Progress. Just makes progress. It's okay to have setbacks and the need for do-overs. It's okay to draw a line in the sand and start over again—and again. Just make sure you are moving the line forward. Move forward. Take baby steps, but at least take steps that keep you from being stuck. Then change will come. And it will be good.[2]

The good news about practice is that you don't have to do it perfectly. That's why it's called practice. So take a deep breath, and release the pressure of having to have this all figured out.

That's not your job. Your job is to practice. It's to imperfectly line up for the kick and give it your best shot again and again and again until you develop the muscles that increase your ability to do this well.

Do the Thing

We've talked about this before, but all real learning happens in the doing and not in the hearing. Just because I've sat in a classroom and listened to teaching doesn't mean I fully understand what I've heard. Medical students spend hours in the classroom as well as hours in labs practicing. Even after they have completed their classroom and lab studies, they are expected to participate in a residency program that lets them perform (practice) in real time with a certified doctor standing right next to them.

Over time, their practice makes permanent—permanent, not perfect. Just this morning I went to the clinic to have my blood drawn. The nurse, who has done this hundreds if not thousands of times, could not get the blood out of my vein. She tried in both arms and then again a third time until she called the nurse practitioner over. At first, the nurse practitioner couldn't get it either. She then took her finger and flicked the tube of the needle. Just like that it began to fill up. She said sometimes, there's just a bubble in there that you have to break up so the blood will come through.

She didn't read that in a textbook. She learned that on-site, and she taught it to the other nurse. You know what will happen next time the first nurse can't get blood to come through? Before she calls for backup, she will flick the tube and see if the air bubble breaks up.

Losing is only losing when there is no learning. Failure is only failure if you don't learn from it. How will you ever know what you can really do if you don't push all the way to failure? The knowledge and relationship you will gain on your side streets and back alleys will be put to the test as you begin to step back onto the old path as a new person. You're not going to get it right every time, but as you move forward, you will figure it out.

This is why the disciples had to make disciples. They not only had to learn and experience Jesus but they had to teach and help others experience Jesus. Their doing solidified their learning. And yours will, too. As you do the work, what you've learned in your head and experienced in your heart will solidify in your life.

There will be times when you don't even realize what you've learned until you hear it come out of your mouth or see it play a role in your choices. It's like claiming how not like your mother you are until that day your kids do something and your mother's words come flying out of your mouth before you can even catch them. And you realize that maybe you are more like your mother than you thought (not that I've ever been in that position).

My friend Lauren is going through some really hard stuff. She and her husband, Matt, have two foster daughters—sisters— who have been with them since birth, or a little over three years. Lauren and Matt have already adopted their older brother. These girls are their girls, and they are their parents. Recently, the girls were placed back in the custody of a close family member since the goal of foster care is always reunification with the birth family, if possible.

Matt and Lauren always knew this was a possibility, but their hearts have been shattered into a million pieces, and they are struggling to move forward. Lauren has been walking the side street of discipleship for more than a year, and in the midst of such dire circumstances, her learning is solidifying.

The other day she called me in the midst of a breakdown. She confessed how angry she was with God and how his goodness in this moment didn't seem so good to her. She recognized this reality of anger when she realized that every time a worship song plays that speaks of God's goodness, she physically cannot sing.

Lauren is allowed to be angry and hurt and confused. But in the midst of her emotions, she is invited to not sin (Ephesians 4:26.) Recognizing and owning her reality was the first part of the battle. She was discouraged over her anger, but at the same time, she wasn't being driven by her anger.

I see so much growth in her emotions. This time last year, she wouldn't have even noticed she was angry. She might have not even realized she wasn't singing during certain songs. Or worse yet, she would be stuffing her feelings down so effectively that she could still sing those songs even though she didn't feel those words.

I'd say that's progress. She's moving forward. She's growing. She's understanding. She's driving her own car. Funny, she called me not only for some insight but also because she figured she wasn't fit to be leading others in discipleship since she was struggling so much with the foundational belief that we have a good, good Father.

"You are exactly who needs to be leading, Lauren. People need to see that it isn't about perfecting this. It's just about doing it. Sometimes, it's going to be easy to believe that God is good, and other times, it's going to be hard. In your case right now, it's really hard. The fact that you are still moving forward in spite of how you are feeling speaks volumes about the God you have come to know. Somewhere deep down, you know he is good, and you know he is kind, and you know how much he really cares. If you didn't, you never would have called."

Lauren is learning, she is growing, she is transforming. This is life. This is discipleship. Sometimes, it will be easy and fun, and other times, it will be hard and unwanted. But always it will be good because always it will be God.

Embrace the Tension

How do you know true change has really taken place? I think the answer is found in new tension, when something happens and you react in a way you would have easily reacted in the past but you notice it, and it feels tense. That's you catching yourself—not enough to not react but enough to notice it. That's progress. Before, you wouldn't have noticed. Now you notice, and noticing is the first step in participating. Before Lauren's transformation, she wouldn't have noticed she wasn't singing. Worse yet, maybe she would have sung the songs and not noticed she wasn't believing the words. The tension in this trial was evidence of her growth, not her failure.

At the Hose House, I learned to see people and not projects. I realized that God cares about relationship more than anything. He loves so deeply. He doesn't get tripped up by sin. In fact, when he sees you, he doesn't even see sin. He sees love. And his love drives him to come in close, even when your heart is far. There will be tension as you learn to embrace the new person you are becoming. Lean into it. Lean into the missteps and failures. Turn away from shame and condemnation. You have no time for that off the beaten path.

Crowds are good and contagious and fun, but God often works in the still, small moments. And no crowd, no matter how welcoming, is better than his presence. Keep journeying, keep practicing, and before you know it, you will find yourself walking in step with the Spirit and doing what you've been created to do, regardless of who is or isn't watching. It's not about platform building or Instagram likes. It's not about thanks or pats on the back. It doesn't matter how the other moms see or don't see you. It's not you trying to win others over or you slaving yourself away in hopes of some acknowledgment. It's just Jesus. It's about authenticity and freedom, faithfulness and calling.

At the end of the day, it's always easier to go back to who you were rather than embrace the work of who you were meant to become. What if I hadn't turned left on my morning run and never faced my shadows head-on? What if I got halfway up the hill only to come back down? What if one of the shadows proved to be too much and I changed my mind about changing my mind?

What if? I think I would have kept running, and God would have kept inviting. I don't think he would ever give up. He will never force me to turn, but he will also never let me settle for less than all he has to offer.

Matthew 3:8 says, "Produce fruit in keeping with repentance." Your fruit will come as you keep with it. Practice makes permanent. You've totally got this.

CHAPTER FIFTEEN

Helping Others Turn Left

Ministry is not about what you do, as much as it is about who you are. And once you find out who you are, everything you do in life has the potential and capacity to be ministry.

—Eric Johnson

Just like my friend Lauren's story, this discipleship journey isn't only about who you are becoming. It's also about who you are helping others become. You are here, reading this book because someone, somewhere made an investment. None of us have happened here all alone. Someone influenced you to walk in this direction. You are a product of other people.

For this to be true, discipleship cannot only be about becoming a disciple. It must also involve paying it forward. Jesus did not just invite one person. He did not just invite two. He invited a group of people, and those people invited people, and those people invited people. The early church started because everyone invited people.

There are people everywhere waiting for help to turn left. They are people who know and sense the invitation of the Father but don't have the courage or understanding to turn and follow. Your journey will give them strength. And you don't even have to be far into it. I wasn't a month into quitting my job before people started calling me with questions about the tension they were also experiencing about invitations from the Father. How did I turn and follow when I didn't know where we were going? Where did I find the courage? How was God taking care of me? What about those I'd left behind?

I was constantly amazed over the power of sharing my story. Each time I recounted all God had done to get me where I was, I grew stronger, more confident, and more excited about what God was going to do. The increased strength wasn't an accident. Testimony is meant to spur one another on.

> *They triumphed over him by the blood of the Lamb and by the word of their testimony.*
>
> —Rev. 12:11

The enemy tried to silence me. On hard days he would work to convince me my stories weren't any good and my journey wasn't worth telling. But the more I shared about God's faithfulness, the more I believed in God's faithfulness. There will be days you struggle more than others, days when you wonder if the work of your left turn is really worth the hassle. On those days, instead of telling stories of what God isn't doing, try recounting what he is doing. Remind your feelings that you have an ever-present, always-faithful Father who cares more about their future than they do.

I found so much strength in telling others about the things God was teaching me. Sometimes, I didn't fully understand all I was learning, but it never mattered. Something about saying it out loud often brought more clarity and understanding. God is a multiplier; he works in us and through us. I think there are times the Father tells us things because he trusts us to say them out loud.

I had a dream the other night. It wasn't anything big, but it involved an old friend of mine who is in ministry on the other side of town. Outside of ministry events, she isn't someone I talk to a lot, but I so vividly remembered this dream that I couldn't help but wonder if I was supposed to share it with her. I pushed it aside and started in on my day.

The thought crossed my mind again over lunch, and I wondered if maybe the Father gave me this dream because he trusted me to share it. And what was the worst thing that could happen? She could tell me I'm off and that it means nothing, and I would be out nothing. As I ate my salad, I looked her up on social media and sent her a message with the contents of my dream.

It wasn't 30 minutes before I received a message back from her telling me how meaningful this dream was to her and how desperate she was to hear some encouragement from the Father. Without telling me a lot of details, she expressed how she found hope in all I shared.

The more you share your story, the more opportunity you will get to share your story. Sometimes, people will listen and receive, and other times, they will put up a wall and reject. Their response is not your responsibility.

Worship at the Hose House

I'm not going to lie, inviting people to join us for worship at the Hose House that happened to be next to a brothel was a little fun. It was especially fun when people within earshot turned their heads, confused over what they thought they might have heard. Testifying about all God was doing steadied my feet in this unknown terrain.

Ella said something to me the other day that relates to this. She's been studying for finals all week and asked if she could invite a bunch of friends over so they could study together. "Mom, for some reason, when I talk it through with my friends, I understand it better." She thought it was funny that she could sit with a teacher and go over history or geometry and walk away a little better off, but when she sat and worked through it with her friends, she inevitably would understand it.

Her friends don't know much more than she knows. For the most part, they are all learning together. The understanding comes in the interchange. It is in the back and forth, the reasoning, the speaking out loud and putting it out there. If we have to have it all figured out before we open our mouths, then we simply aren't going to figure much out in life. Our internal figuring often comes just on the other side of our external processing.

The Reality of Being Real

The reality of being real is where you find the Father. Partnering with authenticity and vulnerability only when it benefits us doesn't work. Anyone can use their weakness when their weakness ends up working in their favor.

Let me try to give you an example. As a speaker and author, I spend a lot of time telling stories. Anything in my life that happens is up for grabs. I am my family's worst nightmare. My girls have a love-hate relationship with having their stories told on stages all over the place. When I speak, I sometimes find it easy to be vulnerable, and sometimes I do not.

Vulnerability is easy for me when I already know the outcome—for instance when I tell a story of a time I struggled to trust God and in my struggle called out to a friend who, in turn, strengthened my resolve and helped me do what I thought I couldn't do. In this story, I am sharing with people about my struggle to trust, but I am also sharing how it all works out in the long run.

It is much harder to be vulnerable in the middle of the mess. When my story becomes a present-day example, it stops being a story and starts being real life. Suddenly, instead of someone standing up front who has figured something out, I am just like those listening, on a journey in which I don't know the way. True vulnerability is being the same with our story whether it benefits us or not. There are stories I need to share about my failures and my faults, stories about my struggle and my unbelief, and I need to share them before I understand them—right in the middle of the mess of it all.

Why? Because it's not actually my story I'm telling. It's God's. I am a participant in the divine story of Christ in me. Every part of my life is an opportunity to share and show Jesus. People don't need to just see how it works out in the long run; they need to see how it's working out in the messy middle—when it hurts, when it doesn't make sense, when you don't understand, when God asks you to do something you don't want to do.

How to Help Others Turn Left

Jesus is the best guide. He is patient and kind, loving and inviting. He doesn't condemn or shame us when we slip up. He's not shocked when we get it completely wrong. He is steady and consistent, and the more you come to know him, the more you are able to follow him as you journey off the beaten path.

Discipleship is necessary because it helps us as we navigate the unknown. When I first started noticing the present work of Holy Spirit, I didn't really know what to do with it. Holy Spirit had always been someone we mentioned more than someone we interacted with on a daily basis. I didn't know what I didn't know until I found people who knew what I didn't.

When Dave and I first joined the staff at the Cincinnati Vineyard Church, we thought it was about what we had to offer. Dave was hired as the elementary pastor, and eventually, I joined the student ministry team. We worked hard to be fruitful there, but upon leaving, I realized that our time there had not been about all we had given the Vineyard as much as it was about all the Vineyard had given us.

Over the course of our time there, we were introduced to a new level of intimacy with Holy Spirit. I'm leaving off *the* in front of Holy Spirit on purpose. You might automatically read it and be most comfortable saying it as the Holy Spirit. There's nothing wrong with saying it that way. Actually, it's more normal than the way I am saying it.

But here's why I leave off *the*. Over the course of our eight years at Cincinnati Vineyard, I discovered and developed an intimate relationship with Holy Spirit. He stopped being an inanimate object and became an intimate friend. I would never say that *the* Jesus was talking to me the other day.

Jesus was here for the disciples. He led them and guided them through the ups and downs of their left turns, and then when he left, he told them it was for their benefit that the One who followed him would prove to be even more useful.

Holy Spirit is our personal guide. He is our companion, our friend, our counselor, our wise mentor. He knows what we don't and has been where we've never been. And his hope is to share all he is with us. He knows the way to the Kingdom, and he's been gifted to us as a guide to find our way.

That being said, I didn't figure all this out on my own. The Vineyard Church was full of people who knew him in a way I didn't. They got my attention the way they talked about Holy Spirit and the way they prayed and worshipped. I noticed how freely they followed and found security in what they didn't know. It was endearing, so I asked for help. I simply found people who had what I wanted and asked them to show me how to get it.

My journey off the beaten path solidified so many round table discussions I had with mentors from the Cincinnati Vineyard. People just like me were doing their thing day in and day out, and along the way, they were willing to share what they'd gained.

This is discipleship—sharing your life over and over again. It's realizing you have the keys to walk through this door, and now you can go back, grab someone's hand, and walk them through it much easier than they can figure it all out alone. As you help others turn left, you will get it wrong. Remember, we've already learned that this does not mean that you will always get it right. Your failure doesn't stop the journey. You do not have that kind of power. God's got this. It's his plan and his invitation, and you walk in his power.

Speak the Good News

It's easy to speak the bad news, so easy that most people do it all the time. We know by now that it's God's kindness that leads us to repentance. His goodness brings us around, and his gentleness invites us to turn and follow. The best way to help others as they try to turn is to listen for the voice of the Father. What is he saying? What isn't he saying?

Sometimes, in the noise of chaos, we struggle to find our center, and thus God's voice is muffled. The condemnation of the enemy is so loud that it can sometimes bring even more confusion to chaos. Discipleship provides us the opportunity to lean in and listen well for the Father on behalf of others.

I sat with my friend from the gym the other day, and somehow we got on the subject of church. She hung her head low and began to say things like this: "I know I need to go back to church. I shouldn't be avoiding it. I need to be growing. It's just that every time I go, I feel like people are judging me for not having been there. Travel and sports make it hard, and I honestly don't know how to better manage them both. I really have to figure out my schedule."

And all of this is true. She does need to be connected to a body of believers. She does need to learn to navigate the tension between weekend sports schedules and family worship, but what isn't true is that she needs to do all of it to not feel ashamed. And the truth is, she could do all of the above and miss the Father in the same way. It's not about what she does and where she goes. It's about who she is and how she's becoming.

"You know what?" I said. "I actually don't think God is sitting back tapping his foot, waiting for you to get your family to a building called church. I think he is present and working in your everyday life. I think he is at the baseball fields and in the gym, and he's working right now at our table as we talk. Do you need consistent faith-filled community? Absolutely! But the good news to your bad news right now is that your relationship with the Father doesn't have to be put on hold while you figure that out. He is available to you every single day. You just have to notice him."

My words felt light, they felt freeing, and they felt inviting. That's because I spoke the good news of the gospel. I set her free. I let her off the hook. The enemy's shame was doing a good job keeping her away from her church community, and I decided to silence him. Jesus's grace would eventually pull her back in. In fact, she did go back fairly quickly after our meeting, and I have to credit Jesus for that one.

In the past, I would have told her she was right, that she needed to figure out her schedule and get her family to the building they called church, even if I knew she wasn't going there because of community and relationship as much as obligation and religion. I would have sent her because it was what you do, and by partnering with the voice of her accusers, I would have missed the chance to point out the invitation of her Father.

If the news you are speaking over your people is not good, then stop speaking it. People can find the bad news on their own; they need guidance in finding the good news. God is continually and constantly good. He is for us, and his language with us is full of grace and truth. Although God is sometimes firm, he is always faithful to keep his word. He doesn't distance himself from you because of what you do; he is present with you because of who he is.

This was the good news my friend needed to hear. She needed to be released from the pressure and performance mentality and set free by God's grace and truth invitation. I'm confident in his ability to pull her in deeply and connect her richly.

Meet People Where They Really Are

The next thing you can do for people as you encourage them to follow Jesus off the beaten path is to meet them in their reality. God meets us where we really are. He doesn't need us to play pretend. Instead, he invites us to lower our guard and be real with our feelings, even when they are unbecoming and not the least bit true.

We all have our moments when the wind gets too strong and the waves too high, when we lose ourselves to the emotional eruption happening on the inside. Life is sometimes too much. We can't do this anymore.

> *No temptation has overtaken you except what is common to mankind. And God is faithful; he will not let you be tempted beyond what you can bear. But when you are tempted, he will also provide a way out so that you can endure it.*
>
> —1 Cor. 10:13

The temptation, when it all hits the fan, is to turn back, to stop traveling this road and deal with the mess quickly and discreetly the best way we know how.

There will be times on this journey when the Lord will use you as somebody's way out. When they've had all they can handle and just as they start to lose their grip, your hand slides over the top of theirs and hangs on for them. This last-minute rescue was made possible by their real-life unraveling. Had you cut them off before they started to let go, you would have missed the connection to help them.

Nothing surprises the Father. We will not get overreactions when we go to him, mostly because nothing we say worries him. Nothing is too big or too hard or too far gone. Everything under the sun is redeemable. Sometimes, the best gift we can give someone is an invitation to be real and not be met with shock.

When the Pharisees threw the adulterous woman in front of Jesus and demanded that he tell them how to handle her, Jesus didn't jump back and gasp over what this woman got caught doing. He bent down low, looked her in the eye, and gave her the gift of connection in the midst of their condemnation. In that moment, the most important thing was that she knew he cared and didn't condemn her. His love was where her freedom would come, not his overreaction to her ugly reality.

If my girls were to come to me with a mess they had made and, in the midst of their sharing, I gasped, grabbed my mouth, and began to fret, then guess what they wouldn't do the next time something felt big to them. They wouldn't come to me. Instead, they would assume their issue was too big for me and thus take on the responsibility for their own issue, missing my help in the midst of trouble. Let people say crazy things to you, and let your underreaction speak highly of your powerful Father.

Ask Lots of Questions

I used to pride myself on being a good answer-giver. That's what pastors do. We study hard, grow wise, and give answers. That was my story until I sat with someone who asked me really good questions. He asked such good questions that I didn't want to answer. It wasn't that I didn't know the answer; I just didn't want to say the answer out loud.

What does it tell us if Jesus, knowing everything, was still the best question-asker? Does it show you that more times than not it's more important to ask than it is to tell? Does it make you rethink how quick you are to tell your kids what you think they need to hear or remind your spouse of the truth he must have forgotten?

Jesus didn't ask questions because he needed answers. He asked questions because the people needed to hear the answers. If we answer honestly, sometimes the words coming out of our mouths shock us. If we chose to answer dishonestly, then sometimes the tinge inside our souls shocks us. Either way, the right questions can become powerful tools of guidance if we use them properly.

The other day I was leading a huddle (that's what we call our discipleship groups at Anthem House Church). A friend of mine in our huddle was having a really hard time with something going on in her life. From all she had shared, I could make an assumption on how to pray for her, or I could ask. I decided to ask. "Julie, if you had to give me one specific way to pray for you this week, what would it be?"

"I don't know," she answered.

I don't know is actually the only wrong answer she could give me in that moment. I don't know is not something specific I can pray for her. She could have told me to pray for her dog, pray for her car, or even pray for her Aunt Ida's cat, and I would have followed through with it, but she could not tell me, "I don't know."

I don't know means she doesn't have to think. She doesn't have to be in reality. She doesn't have to say what would be helpful. It also means that she doesn't have to feel like a burden by admitting she needs something. It could mean a lot more things depending on the person and their temperament.

Her inability to answer provided the group with insight into what she was actually feeling. She was feeling like a burden, like she needed too much help, too much from her community. She didn't want to need the level of help she needed. That's why she didn't answer. It wasn't because she didn't have an answer but because she didn't want her answer to involve her needing any more help from those around her. Noticing this opened our eyes up to so much more.

Jesus asked somewhere close to 300 questions in the Gospels. It's almost twice as many questions as he was asked. If Jesus, God's Son who knows everything, holds question-asking at such a high value, then we should as well.

Ask questions to understand and not answer.
Ask questions to hear and not respond.
Ask questions to give and not receive.
Ask questions to connect and not condemn.
Ask questions to love and not hate.

You can say, "Help me understand why you feel that way" instead of "I'm sorry you feel that way."

"Tell me more about your struggle" instead of "Let me tell you how to stop your struggle."

"What was that experience like for you?" instead of "Here's what I would have done."

"How can I help you?" instead of "Here's what I'm going to do."

"What do you sense the Father saying to you?" instead of "Here's what I say."

We are quick to prescribe remedies for behavior management and slow to conduct conversations that will mend hearts. Be more intentional about discovering and understanding the why behind people's words and feelings. Discover what is under the waterline because in this place of realness, connection will be made.

In the end, our invitation is to help others turn left. And just as the gospel always does, on the other side of helping, we will discover that we are more blessed than when we started. Our guidance with others often leaves us changed, challenged, and checked. As we guide others on their journey, we are strengthened in ours.

This is the story of discipleship. I invest in you because someone is investing in me. You invest in someone else because I am investing in you. We were created for this reproducible cycle. Jesus's last mandate to his disciples was this:

> *All authority in heaven and on earth has been given to me. Therefore go and make disciples of all nations, baptizing them in the name of the Father and of the Son and of the Holy Spirit, and teaching them to obey everything I have commanded you. And surely I am with you always, to the very end of the age.*
>
> —Matt. 28:18–20

He told them to go and make disciples, not just because there were disciples waiting to be made but because they needed one another. Living out our true identity in Christ will look like living in discipleship. We can't spend time walking off the beaten path with Jesus and not begin to live off the beaten path like Jesus.

Jesus made disciples, and Jesus's disciples made disciples, so the fruit of your left turn will essentially be discipleship.

Let me then welcome you to this lifelong journey of discipleship. I suggest that you make yourself a home here. I've grown quite accustomed to left turns. The Father has big plans for you. He has so many places he wants to show you and ways he will grow you. It will definitely be an off-road experience. But I promise that you won't wish you had stayed on the highway when you get to where you're going. This is the road best traveled. Enjoy it.

Endnotes

Chapter 1

1. Dallas Willard, *The Divine Conspiracy, Rediscovering Our Hidden Life with God* (New York: Harper Collins Publishing, 1998), 303.

Chapter 2

1. Alicia Britt Chole, *Anonymous: Jesus' Hidden Years . . . and Yours.* (Nashville, TN: Thomas Nelson Publishers, 2016), 56.

Chapter 7

1. Gravity Leadership, *Journey 1: Find Your Center.* Gravity Leadership Academy, 20.
2. Ben Sternke, *Journey 1: Find your Center*, Gravity Leadership Academy, 2019, 25.
3. A.W. Tozer, *The Knowledge of the Holy* (New York: Harper-Collins, 1978), 4.

Chapter 8

1. Simon Tugwell, *The Beatitudes: Soundings in Christian Tradition* (Templegate Publishers, 1980), 130.
2. Lysa TerKeurst, *It's Not Supposed to Be This Way* (Nashville, TN: Nelson Books, 2018), 9.
3. Jeff Manion, *The Land Between* (Grand Rapids, MI: Zondervan, 2012), 27.

Chapter 11

1. Judah Smith, *How's Your Soul? Why Everything That Matters Starts with the Inside You* (Nashville, TN: Nelson Books, 2016), 51.
2. Peter Scazzero, *Emotionally Healthy Spirituality* (Grand Rapids, MI: Zondervan, 2014), 44.

Chapter 13

1. Bill Johnson, *Manifesto for a Normal Christian Life*, 2012, 76.

Chapter 14

1. Caroline Leaf, *Switch on Your Brain* (Grand Rapids, MI: Baker Books, 2013), 20.
2. Lysa TerKeurst, *UnGlued: Making Wise Choices in the Midst of Raw Emotions.* (Nashville, TN: Thomas Nelson, 2012), 14.